LOVE LETTERS

Grange & that I am
will flourish than
off the bank more

Everything is

an eternally — I adore

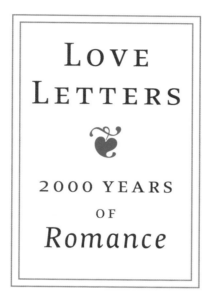

LOVE
LETTERS

2000 YEARS
OF
Romance

EDITED BY
Andrea Clarke

THE BRITISH LIBRARY

In loving memory of my father, David Clarke, 1946–2011

❦

Contents

In an age of emails, tweets and texted 'I luv u's', *Love Letters* invites us into a privileged realm and reminds us why the written word is so special. Drawn from the breadth and depth of the British Library's vast national collection of manuscripts, these handwritten, intimate exchanges between couples – some famous, others now lost to history – span centuries, cultures and continents.

Love letters are, by their very nature, private communications and some of those selected remained a secret between sender and recipient for years, not to be seen, as Margery Brews beseeches John Paston in 1477, 'by any earthly creature save only yourself'. Physically, love letters are like many other manuscript letters, pieces of paper on which there is some writing. However, what makes them compelling to read and imbues them with a magical quality is the emotional bond between the sender and recipient, and, concomitantly, their perceived ability to transform life, transcend time and bridge distances. As Prince Arthur explains to Katherine of Aragon: 'Truly, your letters, traced by your own hand, have so delighted me, and have rendered me so cheerful and jocund, that I fancied I beheld your Highness and conversed with and embraced my dearest wife.'

Love letters are an expression of intimacy; their words allow us insight into the private relationships of people down the ages. The exchanges selected here contain expressions of recognisable human emotions and every shade of love, from the joy of falling in love to the pain of unrequited love. Amorous declarations from across the centuries are included: from the fifteenth century, the young Margery Brews's letter to John Paston, her 'right well-beloved Valentine', declares 'my heart bids me ever more to love you, truly over all earthly thing'; and Pierre Sala's exquisitely illuminated *Petit Livre d'Amour*, which he presented to Marguerite Bullioud, 'who since my childhood I have always wanted to love, serve, esteem and honour'. Gordon Bottomley's declaration of love, sent to Emily Burton in 1899 after five years of friendship, is particularly moving as he declares: 'O, how I hope that I am not estranging you even when I tell you that I love you wholly, that as long as I have known you, you have been to me "half angel and half bird and all a wonder and a wild desire", that your influence alone can waken what is best in me.'

Letters written during courtships also number among the present selection. Dorothy Osborne's charming letter, written in 1653 to her future husband, Sir William Temple, lists the 'great many ingredients that must go to the making me happy in a husband'. In contrast, Charles Dickens's letter to his future wife, Catherine Hogarth, written 'with the greatest pain', just three weeks into their engagement, reveals that he already harboured doubts about their suitability as marriage partners. Amorous exchanges written during passionate affairs also feature. Two love-notes entered in Anne Boleyn's Book of Hours by her and Henry VIII provide some of the earliest evidence for their love affair. The raw passion of love is perhaps best represented in the letter sent by Rupert Brooke to Cathleen Nesbitt, which he ends with the words 'I'm madly eager to see you again. My heart goes knocking when I think of it [...] I will kiss you till I kill you.'

Several of the selected letters are the deeply affectionate out-pourings of tender and happy marriages: Norfolk landowner Thomas Knyvett's delightful letter, sent to his adored wife, Katherine, while away on business in London, to inform her that 'I have been to look for stuff for your bed, and have sent down patterns for you to choose which you like best'; Elizabeth Barrett Browning's sonnet, written for her devoted husband, Robert Barrett Browning, in which she asks 'How do I love thee? Let me count the ways'; and more recently, Mervyn Peake's wonderfully illustrated letter to his wife, Maeve, written shortly before she was due to give birth, in which he simply declares 'Maevie. I am in love. Deeply. Un-endingly, for ever and ever.'

Absence is the subject of several letters, beginning with one written on papyrus in 168 BC by Isaias to her husband, Hephaestion, a soldier in the Egyptian army who has failed to return home to his family. The tone of her letter ranges from loving irritation to incredulity to despair before she ends the letter by entreating him to return home. Katherine Parr, writing as Queen Regent in 1547 while Henry VIII was on a military campaign in France, reminds him that 'whereas I know your Majesty's absence is never without great respects of things most convenient and necessary, yet love and affection compelleth me to desire your presence'.

There is often as much pain and grief in a love affair as pleasure, so it is appropriate that not all the letters in this book point to such happy endings as some of those already mentioned. Among the most heart-rending items in this collection are those that deal with the final separation of loved ones. Tragedy and romance mingle in Sir John Fenwick's letter to his wife, Mary, written in 1697, while awaiting execution for treason. Desperate to see her once more, he implores 'Get to me, if possible, before I die ... All my fear is I shall never see you.' Equally moving is devoted husband and distinguished naval officer Sir Roger Keyes's letter to his wife, Eva, written shortly before he embarked on the dangerous Cuxhaven Raid in December 1914, to ensure that in the event of his death she would know 'how blissfully happy I have been with you my Sweet Red Rose'.

Unrequited love is the theme of other letters in the collection, including Charlotte Brontë's desperate letter to Professor Constantin Héger, in which she confesses that 'truly I find it difficult to be cheerful so long as I think I shall never see you more'. The breath-stopping pain felt by Vanessa in her letter to Jonathan Swift and her sense of separation is real and devastating, as she writes 'Tis impossible to describe what I have suffered since I saw you last; I am sure I could have bore the rack much better than those killing, killing words of yours. Sometimes I have resolved to die without seeing you more; but those resolves, to your misfortune, did not last long.'

The last category of letter included in this selection is the philosophical kind, written by those who reflect back on the end of a love affair. This is perhaps best represented by Oscar Wilde's exquisitely eloquent 50,000-word letter, written from Reading Gaol to his lover 'Bosie', which ends: 'You came to me to learn the pleasures of life and the pleasure of art. Perhaps I am chosen to teach you something much more wonderful. The meaning of sorrow, and its beauty, Your affectionate friend, Oscar Wilde.' Here also belongs the Poet Laureate Ted Hughes's verse-letter, entitled 'Cambridge was our courtship', in which he reflects on his early relationship with the poet Sylvia Plath.

The transcripts of the love letters selected here are all fascinating in their different ways, and paint a vivid picture of each couple – such is the power of words. But, as the accompanying images of the original manuscripts demonstrate, the letters are more than mere collections of words. Having flowed from the hands of the once-living, the letters also have a physical dimension and a palpable story to tell, summed up by Philip Larkin as the 'magical quality of manuscripts'. The physical appearance of the letters can often add another dimension to our understanding, from the revelation of character through handwriting to the actual physical constitution of a letter. Only an image of Margery Brews's letter to John Paston, for example, will reveal upon close inspection that she has made her initials, added to the end of the letter, look like a heart. Similarly, it is only when one sees an image of the original manuscript of Oscar Wilde's 'De Profundis' that one realises it is tear-stained, or that Charlotte Brontë's letters were torn to pieces and then sewn together again, or that Anne Boleyn and Henry VIII deliberately entered their messages to each other beneath highly significant illuminations in Anne's Book of Hours. It is far more poignant to see Emma Hamilton's handwritten, anguished note – 'Oh miserable wretched Emma, oh glorious & happy Nelson' – on his final, unfinished letter to her than it is to read it in a transcript. Looking at an image of the manuscript of the Earl of Essex's impassioned, noble letter to Elizabeth I, with its fold-lines still visible, one starts to imagine the queen loosening its silk ties, breaking the wax seal, and unfolding the letter...

The present selection of love letters are all survivals from the past, and their survival also tells a story; some of them we know, others we are left to imagine. While we can only speculate, for example, that Hephaestion returned to Isaias in such haste after receiving her letter that he left the papyrus behind in the temple, where it was discovered centuries later, we *do* know that Robert Browning treasured the tiny notebook containing Elizabeth Barrett Browning's *Sonnets from the Portuguese* long after her death. Similarly, following the loss of his beloved wife, Emily, Gordon Bottomley treasured their correspondence, sealing each letter in envelopes that would remain unopened for decades, before their purchase by the British Library. As the image on page 111 shows, the envelope in which Roger Keyes enclosed his letter to his wife, Eva, happily reveals that he survived the First World War and that Eva eventually read the letter at his request in 1944, after a long and happy marriage. Somewhat more tragically, Catherine Dickens carefully preserved the letters she had received from her husband, Charles, both before and after marriage, so that 'the world may know he loved me once'. One suspects that similar reasons might have prompted Mme Héger to reconstruct and preserve Charlotte Brontë's letters to her husband, Professor Héger. Taken together, these love letters demonstrate that lovers' preoccupations have changed very little over the last 2000 years, whatever the historical context. Feelings of joy, passion, jealousy and sadness, hope, longing, despair and contentment ruled the human heart and mind, then as now. To read these carefully crafted survivals of the past in an age in which news and feelings seldom travel slowly in the post, will remind us that there is simply nothing quite like receiving a handwritten letter from the one you love. 🖤

'I and the child think of you always ... I entreat you to return'

At the beginning of her letter, Isaias addresses Hephaestion as 'brother', probably by convention, though consanguineous marriages were not unknown in Egypt. It has been conjectured that Hephaestion was a soldier in the Egyptian army who, with a number of his comrades, had sought asylum in the Temple of Serapis at Memphis during the invasion of Egypt by the Syrian king, Antiochus Epiphanes. In July 168 BC Antiochus was forced to retire from Egypt, and at this point Hephaestion's wife, Isaias, would naturally have expected to be quickly reunited with her husband. Evidently, Hephaestion had still not returned home when Isaias was informed that he had been released from the Serapeum. Indignant, she wrote this letter, scolding him for deserting his family, informing him of the difficulties she had faced without him and entreating him to return home. She ended the letter with the softening clause: 'Please take care of yourself.' The letter, written on papyrus, was discovered in the temple, possibly left behind in haste when Hephaestion hurried home to his wife and child. 🍏

Isaias to her brother [husband] Hephaestion, greeting.

If you are well, and your affairs are prospering, it would be as I continually pray to the gods. I myself and the child and all the household are in good health and think of you always. When I received your letter from Horus, in which you explained that you were in sanctuary in the Serapeum at Memphis, I immediately gave thanks to the gods that you were well. But the fact that you did not return with all those who were shut up with you distresses me, for having steered myself and your child through such bad times, and having been

driven to the last extremity because of the high price of corn, I thought that now at least, with you at home, I should get some respite. But you have not given a thought to coming home nor given any regard to our circumstances, knowing how I was short of everything even before you left, not to mention how much time has since passed and such difficult times at that, during which you have sent nothing. And now that Horus, who has delivered your letter, has announced that you have been released, I am utterly distressed. Your mother is also anxious. For her sake as well as mine, I entreat you to please return to the city, unless something more urgent detains you. Please take care of yourself. Farewell.

ΙϹΑϹ ... ΤΩΙ ΑΔΕΛ...
ϹΙ ΕΡΡΩϹΘΕ ΝΤΩΙ ... ΑΛΛΗΤΑ ...
ΑΠΑΝΤΩΝ ΕΙϹ ... ΑΝ ΤΟΙϹ ΘΕΟΙϹ ΕΡΧΟ
ΜΕΝ ... ΤΕ ... ΝΙ ... ΕΠΙ ... ΜΟΝ
ΛΗ ΠΟΤΕΝ ... ΩΝ ... ΟΙ ... ΚΑΙ ΤΟ ...
ϹΟΥ ΑΙ ΑΤΩ ... ΟϹ ... ΑΝΤΟΝ ... ΠΕ ... ΟΙ
ΚΟΥΟ ΜΕΝ Η ... ΠΕΝΤΟΡ ... ΟΥ ...
ΤΟΡΑΓΟϹ ΕΝ ΤΩ ΔΙΕΑΓ ... Ε ... ΩΝ ...
ΕΝ ΚΑΤΟΧΙ ... ΕΝ ΤΩΙ ϹΕΡ ... ΕΩϹ ...
ΕΝ ΤΗ ... ΦΕΙ ΕΤΟ ΠΕΝ ΤΩΙ ΙΕΡ ... Ω ...
ΕΤΟϹ ΕΩϹ ... ΤΟΙϹ ΘΕΟΙϹ ΕΥ ... ΡΙϹ ... ΟΥΝ
ΕΠΙ ΔΕ ... Ω ... ΗΝ ... ΑΠΝΕΛΩΝ ΕΕ
ΤΩΝ ΕΚΑ ... ΕΙ ... ΟΤ ... ΕΝ ΩΝ ΤΩ ...
ΑΝΑ ... ΟΤΩΝ Ε ... Λ ... ΟΥ ΕΚΤΟ ...
ΚΛΗΡΟϹ ... ΟΥ ... Ι ... ϹΕΚΛ ... ΟΤΟ ...
ΔΙΛΚΕΚ ... ΕΡΝΗ ΚΑΙ ... ΚΛΗ ΕϹΤΟ ΑΝΤΙ
ΕΝ ... ΤΩΝ ... ΔΙΛ ... ΤΩΝ ΟΤ ... Ο ...
ΚΑΙ ... Η ... ΑΝ ΕΤΟ ...
ΤΕΥϹ ... Ϲ ... ΩΝ ... ΤΑ ΑΝΑ ΨΥΧΙ ... ΟϹ ...
ΠΙΤΩ ... ΕΝ ... Ε ... ΤΟ ΤΟΔΑΛΥ ... ΕΝ Ε ...
ΠΗϹ ΔΕΝ ... Ε ... ΑΝ ΕΙϹ ΤΗΝ ... ΠΕ ΤΕΡ ... Η ...
ΩϹ ΕΠΙ ... ΤΟ ... ΤΑ ... ΤΟ Ν ... ΩϹ ...
ΠΙ ... ΟΠΙϹ ... ΤΑ ... ΧΗΡ ... ΕΝ ... ΟΥ ...
ΚΑΙ ... ΦΟΡ ... ΟΝ ΚΕΙΡ ΩΝ ΠΙ ... ΕΝ ΤΟ ...
ΕΠΙ ΔΕ ... ΟΝ ... ΗΝ ΕΠΙ ... ΟΛΗ ΝΤΟ ... ΚΕΚ
ΤΙ ΚΩ ... ΟϹ ... ΤΕ ... Ε ΚΑΓΟϹ ... ΠΕΡ ... Ο ...
ΕΚ ΤΗϹ ... ΟΚΛΗ ... ΩΝ ΤΕ ... ΔΗ ... ΟΝ ...
ΕΥ ΤΗΝ ... ΩΝ ... ΕΤΙ ... ΚΑΙ ΤΟ ... Ε ΤΗΟ ...
ΔΟΡΕϹ ΕΧΟΝ ... Ο ... ΟΤΟΙ ΚΑΙ ΠΕ ...
ΚΑΙ ... Ε ... ΟΝ ... ΔΙ ... ΑΝΤ ...
ΑΝ ... ΔΟ ... Ο ... ΕΔΕ ... ΛΗΝ
... ΥϹ ... ΕΠΙ ... ΜΕΝ ... Ν ...

Ryght reverent and worsshypfull lord my...
wheche I beseche almyghty god long f[or]...
in good heole of body ... of herte ...
I desyr it not ... And my lady ...
... for ye wheche god knoweyth I d...
hade not halfe ye lyscolede ...
me to kepe ... tyme whan ... go / I ...
say y I do ... ye ... schalle not ...
be now so myoth ... tyst it schall ...
kepyng And I beseche zow y...
at ... w[i]t full hony herte ...

Feb. 1476.7.   16 E iv.

'My heart bids me ever more to love you, truly over all earthly thing'

The 'Paston letters' are the most famous surviving collection of private correspondence from fifteenth-century England. Over one thousand in number, and dating from 1420 to the end of the fifteenth century, the letters present an incomparable picture of middle-class life during one of the most turbulent periods in English history. Although they are primarily business letters, some deal with courtship and marriage.

In this famous letter, Margery Brews reveals the depth of her love for John Paston III, whom she addresses as 'my right well-beloved Valentine', and expresses her sorrow at the bitter family dispute over the size of her dowry. For although Margery Brews, daughter of Sir Thomas Brews, came from a distinguished family, the match between her and John was embittered by her father's demand for a richer dowry than John had intended to offer. All obstacles were eventually overcome when John's mother, Margaret Paston, gave the couple the manor of Sparham, and the marriage took place before the end of 1477. A decade later, John Paston III fought at the battle of Stoke to defend the new Tudor dynasty against the promoters of the pretender, Lambert Simnel, and was knighted on the field. John and Margery's eldest son, William, born in 1478, was also knighted and became a prominent figure at the court of Henry VIII. 🐦

Feb. 1476-7. 16 E.iv.

Right Reverend and worshipful and my right well-beloved Valentine,
I recommend me unto you full heartily, desiring to hear of your welfare, which
I beseech Almighty God long to preserve unto His pleasure and your heart's
desire. And if it please you to hear of my welfare, I am not in good health either
of body or heart, nor shall I be till I hear from you for there knows no creature
what pain I endure. And even on pain of death I dare it not reveal. And my lady
my mother has pressed the matter on my father full diligently, but she can no
more get than you know of, for which God knows I am most sorry. But if you love
me, as I trust verily you do, you will not leave me therefore. For if you had not

half the livelihood that you have, and if I had to do the greatest labour that any woman alive might, I would not forsake you. And if you command me to keep me true wherever I go I will do all my might to love you and no one else. And if my friends say that I do amiss they shall not hinder me from doing so. My heart bids me ever more to love you, truly over all earthly thing. And if they be never more angry, I trust it shall be better in time coming. No more to you at this time, but the Holy Trinity have you in keeping. And I beseech you that this letter be not seen by any earthly creature save only yourself. And this letter was written at Topcroft with full heavy heart.   By your own M. B.

...pacio dūcūt vrā Subl.̄q̄ teneor / q̄ntū
a pcrastinatio vrī ad me aduentū. Habeo
q̄ huic meo tā ardenti ĩ sē amorj: tā amater
oro vt cepit / et sicuti ego suī noctes et dies
uoqz et Ipsa meū recens noniē ĩ suo sp pctore
tū maturet: vt ex absentibz sīmq pntes: et con
ṡerata gaudia suos aliq̄ado fruct9 decerpat.
ꝛitas Iniūxit) sū exequt9 ĩ comendanda scilicet
ꝫ parentibz meis / atqz ĩ declaranda filiali vrā
quidez sint Illis pgratū audire (me poti9 /
qz obsecro vre quoqz Cel.̄ᵐ mutuas ĩ hoc
ldere: et Ser.̄ᵐⁱˢ Dñis meis vris parētibz me
. Eos aut no secus q̄ᵐ si mei propriȷ pare
or. et obseruo. atqz Illis felicia et ꝓspa cūcta
tas felix et fausta sit. Leta qz sese seruet et
crebro et sepe me uisere velit. quod est futu9
Castello meo Ludlo iiȷ Nonas octob. Anno. 1499

amātissim9 Sponsus et Arthur9 princeps et
Wallie dux coumbie et Restus primogenit9

'And let your coming to me be hastened, that instead of being absent we may be present with each other'

In August 1497, the ten-year old Prince Arthur, eldest son of King Henry VII and Elizabeth of York, was formally betrothed to Katherine of Aragon, daughter of Ferdinand and Isabella of Spain. The marriage by proxy took place at the ancient palace of Woodstock in Oxfordshire, with the Spanish ambassador, Pedro de Ayala, standing in for the bride. Katherine was due to travel to England in 1499, but her departure was delayed by disputes between Henry VII and Ferdinand over the payment of her dowry and by the insecurity of the Tudor dynasty. This is one of several love letters that Arthur sent to Katherine, his 'dearest spouse'. Writing in Latin, Arthur thanked her for her sweet letters and confessed an earnest desire to see her: 'let your coming to me be hastened, that instead of being absent we may be present with each other, and the love conceived between us and the wished-for joys may reap their proper fruit'. Two more years, however, were to elapse before Katherine would travel to England and Arthur would meet his bride-to-be. They were eventually married in Old St Paul's Cathedral on 14 November 1501. Five months later, Arthur, a weak and sickly boy, died at the age of fifteen. Katherine would remain in England to become the wife of his brother Henry, the future Henry VIII – a union that would have the most profound consequences for both the king and England. 🍎

Most illustrious and most excellent lady, my dearest spouse, I wish you very much health, with my hearty commendation.

I have read the most sweet letters of your Highness lately given to me, from which I have easily perceived your most entire love to me. Truly, your letters, traced by your own hand, have so delighted me, and have rendered me so cheerful and jocund, that I fancied I beheld your Highness and conversed with and embraced my dearest wife. I cannot tell you what an earnest desire I feel to see your Highness, and how vexatious to me is this procrastination about your coming. I owe eternal thanks to your excellence that you so lovingly correspond to this my most ardent love. Let it continue, I entreat, as it has begun; and, like I cherish your sweet remembrance night and day, so do you preserve my name ever fresh in your breast. And let your coming to me be hastened, that instead of being absent we may be present with each other, and the love conceived between us and the wished-for joys may reap their proper fruit.

Moreover I have done as your illustrious Highness enjoined me, that is to say, in commending you to the most serene lord and lady King and Queen my parents, and in declaring your filial regard towards them, which to them was most pleasing to hear, especially from my lips. I also beseech your Highness that it may please you to exercise a similar good office for me and to commend me with hearty good will to my most serene lord and lady your parents; for I greatly value, venerate, and esteem them, even as though they were my own, and wish them all happiness and prosperity.

May your Highness be ever fortunate and happy, and be kept safe and joyful, and let me know it often and speedily by your letters, which will be to me most joyous.

Your Highness' loving spouse, Arthur, Prince of Wales,
Duke of Cornwall, & Eldest son of the King.
Ludlow Castle, October 5, 1499

'... you who since my childhood I have always wanted to love, serve, esteem and honour'

This charming 'little book of love' is one of the most personal and intimate manuscripts to have survived from the Renaissance. It was commissioned in about 1500 by Pierre Sala, a courtier and man of letters from Lyons, as a love-token for Marguerite Bullioud. Pierre and Marguerite had in fact been childhood sweethearts, but went on to marry other people. By 1500, however, they were both widowed and so Sala conceived the book, as he explains in its dedicatory letter, to offer to Marguerite as a symbol of his desire to regain her heart. The rest of the volume consists of a collection of love poems that Sala wrote for her, and then had embellished by an artist. The first miniature is the most personal illustration in the manuscript. It depicts Sala placing his heart inside a marguerite flower in the centre of a bed of pansies (pensées), symbols of thoughts and dreams. Sala's accompanying verse reads: 'My heart wishes to be in this marguerite; it will be there despite what envious persons may say; it will always be in my thoughts because it is the queen of flowers.' Beneath the verse, the initial M of Marguerite is formed from a pair of draughtsman's compasses, the traditional symbol of Renaissance lovers. Pierre Sala and Marguerite Bullioud were finally married in around 1515–19; meanwhile the manuscript continues to bear testament to their enduring love. 🍃

To you my dearest and most honoured lady, Madame [...], you who since my childhood I have always wanted to love, serve, esteem and honour to the best of my ability more than any other lady alive for the great qualities you possess, as the most illustrious and most perfect, she who, in my opinion, has always surpassed all others in feeling, honour and worth, since in your person are to be found all the fine qualities one could wish for in a woman. Your most humble and loyal servant, who forever wishes to consider you as his sole lady and

mistress with all his heart and as humbly
as is possible, commends himself to your
kindly grace, informing you that the great
sweetnesses, beauties and courtesies
with which your noble body is replete are
constantly before his eyes or in his thoughts;
therein they obstinately remain and for
this reason he is constantly reopening and
aggravating the incurable wound you
inflicted upon him in the past, from which

he cannot be healed and which leads him to endure and suffer much sorrow
and pain – suffering he gladly bears most uncomplainingly and patiently since
it comes from you from whom he would rather receive pain and torment than
pleasure and joy from any other, because you alone are his succour, his well-
being and his nourishment; you are the only medicine which can cure him if
you so wish. [...] Therefore I clench my hands and beseech you, my sole lady and
mistress, that my situation which is so pitiful be restored and swiftly remedied
by your feeling lest you long repent it. And, in order to refresh your memory,
I am sending you this little book containing pictures and words which are the
two ways by which we can enter the house of memory, since pictures are for the
eye, and words are for the ear, and both make past things seem as if they were
present. And thus, since by means of these two things we can make present what
is absent, and since in the course of the long period of waiting of which you are
the cause, your good servant has somewhat lost track of this noblest memory,
may these pictures and words put him back on the path so surely that he might
never leave it again.

'Be daily prove you shall me find To be to you both loving and kind'

With the exception of Henry VIII's love letters to Anne Boleyn, now held in the Vatican Library, this Book of Hours provides one of the most evocative pieces of evidence for Henry's love affair with Anne. Produced in around 1500, this sumptuously illustrated devotional text was presented to the British Museum in 1823 by King George IV as part of the library of King George III. Very little is known for certain about the manuscript's previous ownership, but, in light of the intimate nature of the notes that Henry and Anne wrote in it to each other, it seems very likely that it did once belong to Anne. Henry chose to write his note to Anne on a page depicting the man of sorrows, thereby intentionally presenting himself as the lovesick king. He wrote in French: 'If you remember my love in your prayers as strongly as I adore you, I shall scarcely be forgotten, for I am yours. Henry Rex forever.' Anne responded with a couplet in English: 'Be daily prove you shall me find / To be to you both loving and kind.' Anne's choice of page was also highly significant, for she wrote her message below an image of the Annunciation, with the Archangel Gabriel telling the Virgin Mary that she would bear a son. By association, Anne was telling Henry that she would succeed where his first queen, Katherine of Aragon, had failed and provide him with the son and heir that he so desperately longed for. 🍎

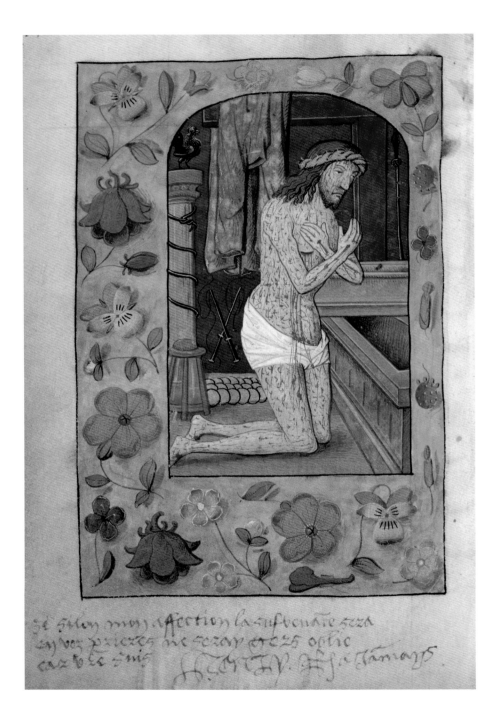

sé selon mon affection la suffisante sera
en vos prieres ne seray erezs ophe
caz ble mis ....

If you remember my love in your prayers as strongly as
I adore you, I shall scarcely be forgotten, for I am yours.
Henry Rex forever.

Be daily prove you shall me find
To be to you both loving and kind.
(Anne Boleyn)

of herited eny fyrst these wordes not to be only
most truely impressed in the hert, muche more
home to go aboute to prayse my self, or exalte
to do I mynde nothyng lesse, but playne symplye
to be towarde your majestye procedyng, the from
wherin I must nedes confesse I deserve no
y, havyng suche Juste occasion to do the same
wythe your majestye, as I do wythe god for
heped upon me dayly, knowlegyng my self a
nto hym in that I do omytt my dutye toward
to recompense the lefte of god benefytes, in whyche
bme to dye, but yett I hope in grmeasons accept
And eyen suche confydence I have in your
vyng my self never to have done my dutye
te to suche a noble and worthy prynce, at whose
nd receyved so muche lode and kyndnes, that whyche
yt; lest I sholde be to tedyouse unto your majestye,
o letter, commyttyng you in to the governance of the lorde
felycite here, & after thys lyf to enioy ' kyngdome of hy

By your majesties humble Kateryn the Qwene KP
obedyent lovyng wyfe &
servant

'God, the knower of secrets, can judge these words not to be only written with ink, but most truly impressed in the heart'

Henry VIII wed Katherine Parr on 12 July 1543 at Hampton Court Palace, in the presence of his three children, Mary, Elizabeth and Edward. Henry was not the twice-widowed Katherine's personal choice, for she was already in love with the younger and more exciting Thomas Seymour, brother of Henry's third wife, Jane. Nevertheless, Katherine bravely put duty before love and became Henry's sixth and last wife. In July 1544, Henry left the shores of England for his final military expedition to France. Shortly before sailing he appointed Katherine, his bride of barely a year, Queen Regent during his absence. This letter, written to Henry by Katherine after his departure, indicates that their marriage had already grown to be very loving and affectionate. Full of heartfelt pleas for news of the king, Katherine tells Henry that she longs for his presence even though she understands that his absence is necessary. Towards the end of the letter, in order to explain her absolute and submissive love for Henry, the devoutly Protestant queen compares it with her love for God. Just a few months after Henry's death in 1547, Thomas Seymour eventually became Katherine's fourth husband, but Katherine tragically died in 1548, soon after giving birth to their first child. 🍂

Although the discourse of time and account of days neither is long nor many of your Majesty's absence, yet the want of your presence, so much beloved and desired of me, maketh me that I cannot quietly pleasure in anything until I hear from your Majesty. The time, therefore, seemeth to me very long, with a great desire to know how your highness hath done since your departing hence, whose prosperity and health I prefer and desire more than mine own. And whereas I know your Majesty's absence is never without great respects of things most convenient and necessary, yet love and affection compelleth me to desire your presence.

And again, the same zeal and love forces me also to be best content with that which is your will and pleasure. And thus love maketh me in all things to set apart mine own commodity and pleasure, and to embrace most joyfully his will and pleasure whom I love. God, the knower of secrets, can judge these words not to be only written with ink, but most truly impressed in the heart. Much more I omit, lest I should seem to go about to praise myself, or crave a thank; which thing to do I mind nothing less, but a plain, simple relation of my zeal and love toward your Majesty, proceeding from the abundance of the heart. Wherein I must needs confess I deserve no worthy commendation, having such just occasion to do the same.

I make like account with your Majesty, as I do with God for his benefits and gifts heaped upon me daily, acknowledging myself always a great debtor unto him in that I do omit my duty toward him, not being able to recompense the least of his benefits; in which state I am certain and sure to die, but yet I hope in His gracious acceptation of my goodwill. And even such confidence I have in your Majesty's gentleness, knowing myself never to have done my duty as was requisite and mete to such a noble and worthy prince, at whose hands I have found and received so much love and goodness, that with words I cannot express it. Lest I should be too tedious unto your Majesty, I finish this my scribbled letter, committing you into the governance of the Lord with long life and prosperous felicity here, and after this life to enjoy the kingdom of his elect.

From Greenwich, by your Majesty's humble, obedient, loving wife and servant,

Kateryn the Queen.

lesse. Therefore for the honor
fall constant in kindnes, for all
are confest to be perfecte. and so
receaue all wishes of perfect

yor Ma:ties most humble
faythfull and affectionate
seruant.

'... the two windows of your privy chamber shall be the poles of my sphere'

Robert Devereux, 2nd Earl of Essex and stepson of Queen Elizabeth I's favourite, Robert Dudley, Earl of Leicester, first arrived at court in 1584. Within three years the dashing twenty-one-year-old had become Elizabeth's constant companion and reigning favourite at court. At the outset of their relationship it was observed that he 'cometh not to his own lodging til the birds sing in the morning'. In 1587 Essex replaced Leicester as Master of the Horse and over the next decade he obtained several important military offices. It was his failure, however, as Lord Lieutenant of Ireland to suppress Tyrone's revolt that led to Essex being stripped of all his offices and placed under house arrest. Angry at his humiliation, Essex led a rash rebellion that resulted in his being charged with treason and executed on Tower Hill on 25 February 1601. This is one of an extraordinary collection of forty-three remarkably intimate letters from Essex to Elizabeth that chart the course of their relationship from 1590 until Essex's death. Written in October 1591, it dates from the period of his greatest favour with the queen. Following courtly convention of the time, Essex assumes the role of Elizabeth's lover, lamenting his separation from his royal mistress while commanding the queen's army in France, and vows that 'the two windows of your privy chamber shall be the poles of my sphere where, as long as your Majesty will please to have me, I am fixed and unmovable'. 🍏

Most fayre, most deere, and most excellent
soueraygne. the first sute J make unto yr
Matie upon my arrivall, is that yr Matie will
free me from writing to yr of any matter of
busines. my duty shallbe otherwise performe
by advertising my ll: of yr Matie servise of
all thinges here: and yett my affection nott
worsed it tells me that zealous fayre
and humble kindnes an argum̃ enough for
a letter. att my departure J had a restlese des
humbly to disingage my self from this french acco
in my absence J conceave an assurd hope to
do somthing that shall make me worthy of
the name of yr servant. att my returne J
will humbly beseach yr Matie that no caus
butt a great action of yr owne may draw m
out of yr sight. for the 2 windowes of yr
privy chamber shallbe the poles of my
sphere. wher, as long as yr Matie will plea
to have mee, J am fixed and unmoveable:
when yr Matie shall thinke heaven to good for m
J will nott fall like a starr, butt be con
like a vapor by the same sun that dre
me up to such a height. while yr Ma
geves me leave to say J love yr my fai
is as my affection unmatchable. if eue
yr deny mee that liberty. yr may end m
life butt never shake my constancy. for v
the sweetnes of yr nature turned into th
greatest bittornes shall itt be. yt is n
in yr power, (as greatt a Q. as yr are) to

Letter from the
Earl of Essex to
Elizabeth I,
18 October 1591

make me lius r teße. Therfore for the honor
of r sex, shew r selfe constant in kindnes, for all
r other ver tues are confest to be perfect: and so
I beseach r Ma:tie receive all wishes of perfect
happines from

r Ma:ties most humble
Thankfull and affectionate
servant.

Most fair, most dear, and most excellent sovereign. The first suit I make unto your Majesty upon my arrival, is that your Majesty will free me from writing to you of any matter of business. My duty shall be otherwise performed by advertising my Lords of your Majesty's counsel of all things here; and yet my affection not wronged which tells me that zealous faith and humble kindness are argument enough for a letter. At my departure I had a restless desire honestly to disengage myself from this French action. In my absence I conceive an assured hope to do something that shall make me worthy of the name of your servant. At my return I will humbly beseech your Majesty that no cause but a great action of your own may draw me out of your sight. For the two windows of your privy chamber shall be the poles of my sphere where, as long as your Majesty will please to have me, I am fixed and unmovable. When you think that heaven

too good for me, I will not fall like a star, but be consumed like a vapour by the same sun that drew me up to such a height. While your Majesty gives me leave to say I love you, my fortune is as my affection, unmatchable. If ever you deny me that liberty you may end my life, but never shake my constancy, for were the sweetness of your nature turned into the greatest bitterness that could be, it is not in your power (as great a Queen as you are) to make me love you less. Therefore, for the honour of your sex, show yourself constant in kindness, for all your other virtues are confessed to be perfect and so I beseech your Majesty receive all wishes of perfect happiness from

Your Majesty's most humble, faithful and affectionate servant, Essex.
Dieppe, this 18th October

...ad a bodije, for the rest, y geve
...he y am seperated Jn body fare
yett y Leave the better parte off me
...tend thee, w[ch] y know Jn being
...wrly saluting off the will doe the
...west Malle and Vinke y pray
the cannott keepe me Longe fr[om]
kissing thij hands more then
...i[s] 27 off August

he who being absent frome
the is nott wth him selfe

Tho: Balkvanle

'And so I leave thee, kissing thy hands more than a thousand times'

By the time of his appointment in 1595 as military commander on Sir John Hawkins and Sir Francis Drake's ill-fated expedition to the Indies, Sir Thomas Baskerville had enjoyed a distinguished military career. He had served as a captain in the Netherlands under Robert Dudley, Earl of Leicester, and was knighted in recognition of the part he played in the capture of *Bergen op Zoom* in 1588. Before setting sail from Plymouth, Baskerville wrote this letter to his wife, Mary, to inform her of his imminent departure and to warn her not to expect to hear from him until his return. Full of optimism, he told her of their plan to capture the principal galleon of the Spanish treasure-fleet, which had been disabled and was lying at Puerto Rico. The expedition, however, was disastrous almost from the start: Sir John Hawkins fell ill and died at sea off Puerto Rico; the Spaniards were forewarned and the attack failed; and Drake, after a succession of further failures, fell ill with dysentery and died off Porto Bello, Panama, on 28 January 1596. Baskerville buried him at sea and brought the remnants of the expedition back to England. In 1597 Mary accompanied her husband on his last voyage to France, where he died of a fever, just two months after the birth of their first son, Hannibal Baskerville. Thomas Baskerville was buried in the new choir of St Paul's Cathedral, beneath a monument that was destroyed in the Great Fire of London in 1666. 🖋

Sweet Malle, I have now received two letters from thee and answered thee none, but now I will come out of this debt. Thy cousin Chachme I have entertained, who for thy sake (who hath all power of me) I will use as well as my means or fortune will give me leave. We attend only the wind, and therefore you must take this letter as a farewell, for I trust I shall have no opportunity to write to you

more till my return, which I hope shall be in six months or seven at the farthest, but longer than eight I will not take of you, therefore about that time assuredly look for our return. We have received advice that hath put great hopes into us, and that is of a ship beaten into an island in the West Indies by tempest, laden with two millions and a half, which I doubt not by God's help to carry. I leave then to thy judgement whether it be not six months well spent to get such a booty. For the rest, I give thee full assurance that though I am separated in body far from thee by great distance, yet I leave the better part of me, which is my spirit, to attend thee, which I know in bearing the continual company and hourly saluting of thee will do the part of a friend. Farewell, sweet Malle, and think, I pray thee, that my desire to see thee cannot keep me long from thee. And so I leave thee, kissing thy hands more than a thousand times. Plymouth, this 21 of August.

*He who being absent from
thee is not with himself,
Thomas Baskerville*

Sweet malle I have now receaved 2 letters from the and answerd the now butt now I will com owt off this dett, thy cousen Charine I have entertayned for thy sake (who hathe all powre off me) I will vse as well as my meanes or fortune will gett me leave, we atend only the wind and therfor you must take this letter as a farewell for I truist I shall have no opertunitij to wryght to you more till my retorne wch I hope shalbe In sij, monethe or sevin att the farthest, butt lenger then 8 I will nott be off you, therfor abowte thatt tyme ardently loke for owr retowne we have receaved advise thatt have butt great hopes Into vs, and thatt is off a ship beaten Into an Iland In the west Indies by tempest Laden wch to millions and ahalfe wch I dowbt nott by gods helpe butt to carrie, I leave then to thij Judgement w{h}ithr itt be nott sij enowhe well spent to gett such a bootie, for the rest, I gell thee full asurance thatt thowghe I am separatid In body farr from thee by great distance, yett I have the better parte off me wch is my spirrit to atend thee, wch I know In biring the continuelle company and howrly saluting off the will do the parte of a friend, farewell sweett malle and thinke I pray the thatt my desire to see the cannott keep me longe from the, and so I leave the kissing thy hand more then a 1000 tymes plymuthe this 27 of August

he who being absent frome the is nott wth him self.

J: Thos: Baskervile

I have been to
bedde and hand[...]
yanto choose which you like
to the patonrn[...]
you lack any t[...]
company you [...]
me know of [...]
yours the rest
Intreating th[...]
the more merry to think than [...]
had rather b[...]
place vnder [...]

Honborn 26
Nobe: 1622.

'I am forced yet to send the shadow of myself'

Thomas Knyvett of Ashwellthorpe in Norfolk, a direct descendant of Sir John Knyvett, Chancellor of Richard III, married Katherine Burgh, the youngest daughter of Thomas Burgh, 5th Baron of Gainsborough, at Mary-le-Strand in London on 28 February 1620. The couple experienced frequent periods of separation throughout their marriage: in the earlier years on account of legal business that demanded Knyvett's presence in London and, following the outbreak of the Civil War, due to difficulties with the Parliamentary government in which his Royalist sympathies involved him. During his absences from home, Knyvett wrote regularly to Katherine; eighty-eight of his letters have survived, revealing the deep affection between husband and wife that helped them to weather the difficulties and dangers which they faced. Knyvett wrote this letter a year and a half into their marriage, but his affectionate words, his declared impatience to return to Katherine's side and to sleep in her arms, and reference to his careful choice of presents for his wife are all regular features of the other letters. Katherine died at the end of April 1646. Knyvett outlived his wife by more than ten years but did not remarry, and instead focused on finding suitable marriage partners for their four surviving children. He was buried alongside Katherine in 1658 in Ashwellthorpe church. 🍂

*Sweet heart, I am forced yet to send the shadow of myself, the true affection
of a substance that loves you above all the world. My business I hope will be
effectually dispatched presently, and God willing I will be with thee before you
are aware. I have been to look for stuff for your bed and have sent down patterns
for you to choose which you like best, they are the nearest to the pattern that
we can find. If you lack anything except my company you are to blame not to
let me know of it, for myself being only yours the rest do follow. Thus in haste,
entreating thee to be merry, and the more merry to think thou have him in thy
arms that had rather be with you than in any place under heaven. And so I rest*

> *Thy dear loving
> husband forever,
> Thomas Knyvett.*

Sweet harte I am forst to yet to send the
shaddawe of my selfe, the true affection
of a substance that lobes you abone all
the world, my business I hope wilbe effectu
ally dispatcht presently and god wiling
I will be with the before you are aware
I hane been to look for I stufe for y
bedde and hane sent Towne patternes for
you to choose which you like best, thay are the neerest
to the patonrne that wee can finde; if
you lack any thing to my accept my
company you are to blame not to lett
me knowe of it, for my selfe being only
yours the rest doe followe, Thus in hast
Intreating the to be merry and
the more merry to think thou hast him in thy armes that
had rather be with you then many
place under heaven, and so I rest

Honborn 26
Mober: 1622.

Thy deer lobing
husband forever

Tho: Knybett

My deve bad and Gos

Fr imitation of s.t fir
an account of him yo
obedient stout kind
s.r ~~Matthass~~ enve yo
perfectie reconved
three things that
this great busines
for gives ~~and~~ you
nations honor
m selfe that tho
at last

'I have too lately said I love you better than myself'

As both King James VI of Scotland and later as King of England, James I's sexuality and choice of male partners were the subject of gossip from the taverns to the Privy Council. When James inherited the English throne from Queen Elizabeth I in 1603, it was openly joked that *'Rex fuit Elizabeth: nunc est regina Jacobus'* ('Elizabeth was King: now James is Queen'). George Villiers, the son of an impoverished Leicestershire squire, was introduced to the king in the summer of 1614 and in November that year he was appointed the Royal Cupbearer. The following year he was knighted and appointed Gentleman of the Bedchamber and in 1616 created Viscount Villiers. Responding to his Privy Council's remonstrations in 1617, after having elevated Villiers to the earldom of Buckingham, James declared that that he loved Buckingham 'more than any other man'. The king continued to delight in his favourite, whose spectacular rise continued, becoming a Marquis in 1618, Lord High Admiral in 1619 and finally the Duke of Buckingham in 1623. In the same year Buckingham wrote this letter to James from Madrid, where he was engaged in marriage negotiations for Prince Charles, the king's son, to marry a Spanish princess. He addressed the king as 'My dear Dad and Gossip' (chum) and signed himself 'your majesty's humble slave and dog Steenie'. Steenie was James I's nickname for him, a diminutive of Stephen and a Biblical reference to St Stephen, whose face at the moment of martyrdom was said to have been that of an angel. �}

My dear Dad and Gossip,

In imitation of St. John I will give you an account of him you love best after your obedient, stout, kind and discreet son: that's myself. Sir, I assure you I am now so perfectly recovered that there is but three things that troubles me. First, that this great business hath no better an issue for yours, your son's, and whole nation's honour; but in this I comfort myself that though it's late, yet now at last you shall know the truth and know what to trust hereafter to. The second is my absence from you, but in that I have likewise comfort that now I shall be soon with you. The third and last was weariness with looking and casting what presents to give here away; but the pleasure I have now in writing to your Majesty hath also relieved me of that, so that now I want nothing but means how to appear in some degree thankful and worthy of your absent favours. But this is not a work of a newly recovered man out of a sickness; it rather requires a man in perfect health and strength and likely to live hundreds of years. Therefore, my best way is to make much of myself that I may live longer, and methinks I hear you say I thank thee more for that than for service to myself. If the substance of this letter be naught or little worth, I am sure my intentions good and so is the form, for with the same style I began I end: that is, in confidence and love. Yet in one respect

I should be discouraged to do so, for
though you are the best father, master,
and I may with sauciness put in friend,
though it be with an humble heart, yet
when I consider my own defects and
unworthiness and how fruitless a servant
I have been, it makes me with shame and
admiration look both on your Majesty
and your servant. Before Clarke came, I
had thrown off sickness, but the relations
he made of your abundant care of me,
and largely expressed in a letter from
Secretary Conway, hath made me take a
full possession of health, so that though
your favours may say truly in loving you

I love myself, yet the ambition I shall ever have of preserving them with the loss of
life and all other things I have, shall witness I love you with more than a self-love.
Sir, judge whether I have pleasure or not in writing to you, for though I thought to
have made an end on the other side, methinks it's too soon here; but I fear I have
troubled you too long. And I have too lately said I love you better than myself,
so in writing longer to please myself, I should give to what I have already said a
contradiction, wherefore I'll end with craving your blessing.

The nine and twentieth
of August

Your Majesty's humble
slave and dog,
Steenie

My dere dad and Gossope:/

In imitation of S.t fisher I will giue you
an account of him you loue best after your
selfe that is my selfe,
obedient stout kind and discreet some
so f . . . . assewre you f ame now so
perfectle recouered that there is but
three things that troubles me, first that
this great busines hath no better an issew
for yours . . . your sonnes and whole
nations honor, but in this I comfort
my selfe that though its late yett
now at last you shall know the
truth and know what to trust
hereafter to, the second is my absence
from you, but in that f haue likewise
comfort that now f shall be some
with you, the theird and last
was wennes with conning and casting
what presents to giue here away but
the pleasure f haue now in writing to
your ma.tie hath allredie releeued me of
that, so that now f want nothing but
meanes how to asscue . . . in some degre

First and last pages of letter from George Villiers to James I, 29 August 1623

your seruant, before Clarke came I
had throne of sicknes but the relations
he made of your aboundant care of me
and largelie exprest in a letter from
secretarie Coneway hath made me
take a full posseshion of helth, so
that though your fauors may say treulie
in loueing you I loue my selfe yett the
ambition I shall euer haue of preseueing them with
the hass of life and all other things
I haue shall witnes I loue you with
more then a selfe loue, so iudge whe=
ther I haue pleasure or not in writing
to you for though I thought to
haue made an end on the other side
me thinks its to sone here but I fee
I haue troubled you to longe, and I
haue tow late saide I loue you
better then my selfe so in writing longer
to pleas my selfe I should giue to what
I haue allredie said a contradiction
wherefore I'le end with crauing your
blessing

the nine and twentith   your majs humble
of august   slaue and doge
                                        steenie

_uersion and I should sooner hope to gain
_ then upon one that did not consider mee
loue mee (_or hate_); ile swere she is much Easyr to
to bee, there are a great many ingredien_
king mee happy in a husband, first a
our humors must agree _and to doe that he_ must haue_
ng that I haue had and vsed that kinde of co
st not bee soe much a Country Gentleman
_ing but hawks and dog's and _ fonder of
_ife, nor the next sort of _ them _
_no further _then_ to bee Justice of peace and
_ sheriff who read noe book but statut's
_ but how to make a speech enterlarded
y amaze his disagreeing poore Neighbo
_her then perswade _them_ into quietnesse; hee must
_t began the world in a free scoole was sent
vniversity and is at his farthest when he
Court has noe acquaintance but those of
_e placis speaks the french hee has pickt
d admires nothing but the storry's hee has
_t were kept there before his time; hee _
llant neither that liues in a Tauern and a
_t imagin how an hower should bee spent
_se it bee in sleeving that makes court to all _

'... there are a great many ingredients must go to the making me happy in a husband'

During their lengthy courtship, Dorothy, daughter of Sir Peter Osborne, royalist lieutenant-governor of Guernsey, wrote a well-known sequence of over seventy letters to Sir William Temple, son of Sir John Temple, Master of the Rolls in Ireland. Having first met in 1646, when William was due to embark on a five-year tour of the continent, their correspondence finally commenced in the winter of 1652 when William was abroad on a diplomatic mission, and ended in October 1654 when Dorothy was struck down by a severe attack of smallpox that nearly killed her. All kinds of practical difficulties beset the couple. Both families opposed their engagement, due to personal antipathies intensified by opposing political views. Dorothy's father had also hoped for a more lucrative match for his youngest daughter to help restore the family fortunes, which had suffered due to the heavy fines imposed by the parliamentary government for his support for Charles I.

At last, however, all obstacles were surmounted, and the pair married on Christmas Day in 1654. In this letter written the previous year, Dorothy provides William with her definition of the perfect husband. As with all her letters, it is elegantly written and full of a tenderness, vivaciousness and humour that makes it compelling to read. 🍂

Sir, [...] there are a great many ingredients must go to the making me happy in a husband. First ... our humours must agree; and to do that he must have that kind of breeding that I have had and used that kind of company. That is, he must not be so much a country gentleman as to understand nothing but hawks and dogs, and be fonder of either than his wife; nor of the next sort of them whose aim reaches no further than to be Justice of Peace and once in his life High Sheriff, who reads no book but statutes and studies nothing but how to make a speech interlaced with Latin, that may amaze his poor disagreeing neighbours and fright them, rather than persuade them into quietness. He must not be a thing that began the world in a free school, was sent from thence to the university, and is at his farthest when he reaches the Inns of Court; has no acquaintance but those of his form in these places, speaks the French he has picked out of old laws, and admires nothing but the stories he has heard of the revels that were kept there before his time. He must not be a town gallant neither, that lives in a tavern and an ordinary that cannot imagine how an hour should be spent without company, unless it be in sleeping; that makes court to all the women he sees, thinks they believe him, laughs and is laughed at equally. Nor a travelled Monsieur whose head is all feather inside and outside, that can talk of nothing but dances and duels ... He must not be a fool of no sort, nor peevish, nor ill-natured, nor proud, nor covetous; and to all this must be added, that he must love me and I him, as much as we are capable of loving. Without all this his fortune, though never so great, would not satisfy me; and with it a very moderate one would keep me from repenting my disposal. [...] I am yours.

Sr WILLIAM TEMPLE

In the Collection of John Temple Esqr

J. Houbraken sculp. Amst.

P. Lely Pinxit

Impensis J. & P. Knapton Londini 1738.

Tuesda

my dearest life, I ha
morning & all the re
writ ~~———~~ every nigh
have not came as th
doe to take them in
wch is the only time
them, the reason I
but I wonder they ha
you word, dd life, j
yo selfe, & the teare
you is a double dea
take take c

SIR JOHN FENWICK TO HIS WIFE, MARY
JANUARY 1697

'Get to me, if possible, before I die ... All my fear is I shall never see you'

Sir John Fenwick was an army officer and Jacobite conspirator. A strong partisan of King James II, he was briefly imprisoned in 1689 for plotting against King William III, who had ascended the throne in 1688 following the Protestant coup that became known as 'The Glorious Revolution'. In May 1691, Fenwick publicly mocked Queen Mary in St James's Park, an imprudent act that William would not forget. On his release from prison, Fenwick had continued his plotting and in February 1696 his plans for an armed insurrection were discovered, forcing him into hiding. In June of the same year, while attempting to flee to France, Fenwick was arrested. However, the government was unable to produce enough evidence to place him on trial for treason and so it was decided to proceed against him by Bill of Attainder. Fenwick therefore became the last Englishman to be tried for treason and condemned to death by Parliament. His devoted wife Mary tirelessly campaigned to save his life and a number of peers also protested against Fenwick's condemnation; but the king proved inexorable and gave his ascent to the bill on 11 January 1697. Fenwick sent this letter to Mary from Newgate Prison, shortly before his execution on Tower Hill on 28 January 1697. 🖤

Tuesday night

My dearest life, I have yours [letter] of this morning and all the rest, and have written every night, but they have not come as they used to do to take them in the morning, which is the only time I can give them. The reason I know not, but I wonder they have not sent you word. D[earest] d[earest] life, you will kill yourself, and the fear I have for you is a double death to me. For God's sake take care of yourself and destroy not your health. I know it is to no purpose, for nothing but my blood will satisfy this man [i.e. the King]. Get to me if possible before I die, sure he will not be so barbarous to deny that. I fear your petition to the House will do no good but you have better advice than I can give. Pray God give you success in it and that we may yet have a happy meeting. I burned those letters I wrote for I dare not keep them, since I could not send them least I should be searched, and there is an officer in the next room with soldiers with him and a guard under the window who makes such a noise that I can get no

Arrest of Sir John Fenwick

sleep and those in the next room perpetually smoking tobacco that it stinks into this room, that they had as good be in it, but I have none but Ashby in the room with me. [...] I expect every moment to have notice of the dead warrant, and then I suppose I shall be used with all barbarity. All my fear is I shall never see you, and that will make me distracted. If I must die, I should be glad you could get the favour I might be beheaded and not die the other shameful death. I shall want a flannel waist-coat, for these I have is a shame to have me stripped in before all the people, nor have I a whole shirt, these are all rags, one will serve me for that day, and I should have a nightcap of white satin with a Holland one under it turned upon it. I mention these things, but alas at the same time I know you have no money, and how you do to live God knows. It were as well for us both they took my life, for if he keeps me alive, he will seize of all we have, and then we should both starve. Pray God bless my dear Love, and bring you to my arms.

Pages 1, 3 and 4 of letter from Sir John Fenwick
to his wife, Mary, January 1697

with me, I think it not best to complain of it
any 1d: Mungo—can get no rest for them, so
perhaps he may, wch will be best so certainly
such usage was never to a gentleman before
nor souldiers ever put in a county goale wch
is contrary to Law, the Shirriffs wch are all
removed but Ashby, how long he may stay I
know not, I expect every moment to have
notice of the dead warrant, & then I suppose
I shall be used with all barbarity, all my
feare is I shall never see you, & that will make
me distracted, if I must dye I should be glad
you could get the favour I might be beheaded

48503

3

& not dye the other shamefull death, I shall
want a flanell wastcoate for that I have is a
shame to have me swiped in before all the
people now have I a whole shirt, these are all
rags one will serve me for that day, & I should
have a night capp of white satin with a holland
one under it turned upon it, I mention these things
but alass at the same time I know you have
no money & how you doe to live god knows.
It were well for us both they took my life
for if he keeps me alive he will seaze of all we
have & then we shall both starve, pray god
. . . and deare Love, & bring you to my armes

4

67

... as you could. y...
...ld gett the better of your inclinati...
...ften as you remembred there was so...
...if you continue to treat me as you...
...ade uneasy by me long. tis imposs...
I have suffer'd since I saw you to...
...ed have bore the Rack much bet...
...g killing words of yours. some...
...loved to die without seeing yo...
...se resolves to your misfortune d...
...g. for there is something in hu...
...prompts one so to find relieffe in...
...give way to it. and be if you'd...
...kindly to me, for I am sure you...
one to suffer what I have done, coul...
reason if I write to you, is because y...
...should I see you. for when y...
you are angry, and there is some the...
...wful, that it strikes me dumb. oh tha...
...so much regard for me left, that th...
touch your Soul, with pitty. if joy or...

'I could have bore the rack much better than those killing, killing words of yours'

Jonathan Swift's tortured, triangular relationship with 'Stella' (Esther Johnson) and 'Vanessa' (Esther Van Homrigh) was the object of much speculation during his lifetime, and still attracts conjecture today. Born in Dublin in 1667, the author of *Gulliver's Travels* moved to England in 1689 and became secretary to government official Sir William Temple. It was in Temple's household that Swift met his life-companion, Stella, who in 1701 moved to Dublin with her chaperone, Rebecca Dingley, to take up residence near to St Patrick's Cathedral, where Swift had obtained the prebend. It was during a visit to London in 1710 that Swift met Vanessa, the daughter of a Dutch merchant and twenty-one years his junior. They struck up a correspondence and Swift immortalised

his feelings for her in his most famous work of narrative poetry, *Cadenus and Vanessa*. Like Stella before her, Vanessa followed Swift to Dublin and took up residence there, with the result that the two women unwittingly competed for his attention. In this letter, Vanessa bitterly protests at her perceived ill-treatment by Swift and pleads for another meeting. It is said that when Swift finally ended their turbulent affair in 1723, Vanessa died of shock. 🌿

Dublin, 1714

Well now I plainly see how great a regard you have for me. You bid me be easy, and you'd see me as often as you could. You had better said, as often as you could get the better of your inclinations, so much, or as often as you remembered there was such a one in the world. If you continue to treat me as you do, you will not be made uneasy by me long. 'Tis impossible to describe what I have suffered since I saw you last; I am sure I could have bore the rack much better than those killing, killing words of yours. Sometimes I have resolved to die without seeing you more; but those resolves, to your misfortune, did not last long. For there is something in human nature that prompts one so to find relief in this world, I must give way to it, and beg you'd see me and speak kindly to me; for I am sure you'd not condemn any one to suffer what I have done, could you but know it.

The reason I write to you is because I cannot tell you, should I see you; for when I begin to complain, then you are angry, and there is something in your look so awful, that it strikes me dumb. Oh that you may but have so much regard for me left, that this complaint may touch your soul with pity. I say as little as ever I can: did you but know what I thought, I'm sure it would move you. Forgive me, and believe I cannot help telling you this, and live.

Dublin 1714

Well now I plainly see how great a regard
you have for me. you bid me be easy, and you'd see me
as often as you could. you had better said as often as
you could get the better of your inclinations, so much.
or as often as you remembred there was such a one in the
world. if you continue to treat me as you do, you will
not be made uneasy by me long. tis impossible to describe
what I have suffer'd since I saw you last, I am sure
I could have bore the rack much better then those
killing, killing, words of yours. some times I have
resolved to die without seeing you more, but
those resolves to your misfortune did not last
long. for there is something in humain nature
that prompts one so to find relief in this world, I
must give way to it. and beg you'd see me and
speak kindly to me, for I am sure you'd not condemn
any one to suffer what I have done could you but know it.
the reason I write to you, is because I cannot tell it
you, should I see you. for when I begin to complain
then you are angry, and there is something in your look
so awful, that it strikes me dumb. oh that you may but
have so much regard for me left that this complaint
may touch your soul with pitty. I say as little as ever I can
did you but know what I thought I am sure it would move
you. to save me trouble believe I cannot help telling you this long

Victory Oct: 19: 1805
Noon Cadiz ESE 16 Leagues

My Dearest beloved Emma the dear
friend of my bosom the Signal has
been made that the Enemys Combined
fleet are coming out of Port, We
have very little Wind so that I have
no hopes of seeing them before to morrow
may the God of Battles crown my
endeavours with success at all events
I will take care that my name shall ever
be most dear to You and Horatia both
of whom I love as much as my own
life, and as my last writing before the
battle will be to You so I hope in God that
I shall live to finish my letter after the

'... as my last writing before the battle will be to you so I hope in God that I shall live to finish my letter after the Battle'

Lady Emma Hamilton and Horatio Nelson's passionate and adulterous love affair began some time in 1798. It scandalised the same society that revered Nelson for his military prowess, and has fascinated people ever since. During Nelson's long absences at sea, the two lovers had to communicate by letter. Afraid of exposure in the press, however, Nelson was very careful in his language to Emma, addressing her as his 'dearest friend' and never acknowledging the paternity of their daughter Horatia. Nelson also destroyed Emma's letters to him and urged her to do the same with those he sent her, but Emma could not bear to do so and kept every one. Few documents in the British Library's collections are more evocative than this, Nelson's final letter to Emma, which was found unfinished on his desk after he was fatally wounded by a French

musket ball while on the deck of the *Victory* during the Battle of Trafalgar. When the letter was delivered to Lady Hamilton by Captain Hardy, she added an anguished note to the end: 'Oh miserable wretched Emma, oh glorious & happy Nelson.' 🍒

Victory Oct[ob]er 19th 1805 Noon, Cadiz ESE 16 Leagues

My Dearest beloved Emma the dear friend of my bosom, the signal has been made that the enemys combined fleet are coming out of port. We have very little wind so that I have no hopes of seeing them before tomorrow. May the God of Battles crown my endeavours with success, at all events I will take care that my name shall ever be most dear to you and Horatia, both of whom I love as much as my own life. And as my last writing before the battle will be to you, so I hope in God that I shall live to finish my letter after the Battle. May heaven bless you prays your Nelson & Bronte. Oct[ob]er 20 in the morning we were close to the mouth of the Straits but the wind had not come far enough to the westward to allow the combined fleets to weather the shoals off Trafalgar but they were counted as far as forty sail of ships of war, which I suppose to be 34 of the line and six frigates. A group of them was seen off the lighthouse of Cadiz this morning but it blows so very fresh & thick weather that I rather believe they will get into the harbour before night. May God almighty give us success over these fellows and enable us to get a peace.

This letter was found open on his desk and brought to Lady Hamilton by Cap[tai]n Hardy.

Oh miserable wretched Emma
Oh glorious & happy Nelson.

...aven bless you prays
...rente, Oct. 20th; in the
...now to the mouth of the
Wind had not come far
...w to allow the Combined
...Shoals of Trafalgar but
as far as forty Sail of Ships
whose to the 34 of the Line
...a Group of them was
...out of Cadiz this Morn
...very fresh & thick weather
...une they will go into
...e night, May the
...success over these fellows

and enable us to get a Peace

This letter was found open on
his desk & brought to
Lady Hamilton by
Capn Hardy

oh miserable wretched Emma
oh glorious & happy Nelson

...ee of friends and pursuits
...t your side. if you knew
...anxiety with which I wat...
...ess, the joy with which
...recovery, and the eagerne...
...would promote your
...cure more readily und...
...tenth of the pain or
..., but so difficult to

...r yours most affectionately
Charles Dickens.

'The sudden and uncalled-for coldness with which you treated me ... both surprised and deeply hurt me'

In May 1835 Charles Dickens became engaged to Catherine Hogarth, daughter of Charles Hogarth, editor of the *Evening Chronicle*. They were married on 2 April 1836 at St Luke's Church, Chelsea, and in the same month Dickens published the highly successful *Pickwick Papers*. Over the next twenty years the novelist published some of his most famous books, including *Oliver Twist*, *Nicholas Nickleby*, *A Christmas Carol*, *David Copperfield*, *Bleak House* and *Little Dorrit*. Despite establishing himself as the most popular writer in Britain, Dickens was intensely unhappy on a personal level, and had grown increasingly restless and dissatisfied in his marriage to Catherine, who had borne him ten children. In July 1857 Dickens befriended Ellen Lawless Ternan, an eighteen-year-old actress, and the following year was estranged from Catherine in a blaze of publicity. This letter, written just three weeks into Dickens's engagement to Catherine, shows that even before their marriage he had doubts about their compatibility. Although not a love letter proper, it does illustrate the intensity of Dickens's feelings for his wife-to-be, which as he reminded her 'has led me to forget all my friends and pursuits to spend my days at your side'. Catherine carefully preserved the letters she had received from her husband, both before and after marriage, so 'that the world may know he loved me once'. 🖤

My dear Catherine,

    It is with the greatest pain that I sit down before I go to bed tonight, to say one word which can bear the appearance of unkindness or reproach; but I owe a duty to myself as well as to you, and as I was wild enough to think that an engagement of even three weeks might pass without any such display as you have favoured me with twice already, I am more strongly induced to discharge it.

    The sudden and uncalled-for coldness with which you treated me just before I left last night, both surprised and deeply hurt me – surprised, because I could not have believed that such sullen and inflexible obstinancy could exist in the breast of any girl in whose heart love had found a place; and hurt me, because I feel for you far more than I have ever professed, and feel a slight from you more than I care to tell. My object in writing to you is this: If a hasty temper produces this strange behaviour, acknowledge it when I give you the opportunity – not once or twice, but again and again. If a feeling of you know not what – a capricious restlessness of you can't tell what, and a desire to tease, you don't know why, give rise to it – overcome it; it will never make you more amiable, I more fond or either of us, more happy. If three weeks or three months of my society has wearied you, do not trifle with me, using me like any other toy as suits your humour for the moment; but make the acknowledgement to me frankly at once – I shall not forget you lightly, but you will need no second warning. Depend upon it, whatever be the cause of your unkindness – whatever gives rise to these wayward fancies – that what you do not take the trouble to conceal from a Lover's eyes, will be frequently acted before those of a husband.

I know as well, as if I were by your side at this moment, that your present impulse on reading this letter is one of anger – pride perhaps, or to use a word more current with your sex – 'spirit'. My dear girl, I have not the most remote intention of awakening any such feeling, and I implore you, not to entertain it for an instant. I am very little your superior in years: in no other respect can I lay claim to the title, but I venture nevertheless to give you advice first, because I cannot turn coolly away and forget a slight from you as I might from any other girl to whom I was not warmly and deeply attached; and secondly, because if you really love me I would have you do justice to yourself, and show me that your love for me, like mine for you, is above the ordinary trickery, and frivolous absurdity which debases the name and renders it ludicrous.

I have written these few lines in haste, but not in anger. I am not angry, but I am hurt, for the second time. Possibly you may not understand the sense in which I use the word; if so, I hope you never may. If you knew the intensity of the feeling which has led me to forget all my friends and pursuits to spend my days at your side; if you knew but half the anxiety with which I watched your recent illness, the joy with which I hailed your recovery, and the eagerness with which I would promote your happiness, you could more readily understand the extent of the pain so easily inflicted, but so difficult to be forgotten.

Ever yours most affectionately Charles Dickens

First and last pages of letter from Charles Dickens to Catherine Hogarth, May 1835

led me to forget all my friends and pursuits to
spend my days at your side. if you knew
but half the anxiety with which I watched
your recent illness, the joy with which
I hailed your recovery, and the eagerness
with which I would promote your
happiness, you could more readily under=
stand the extent of the pain so
easily inflicted, but so difficult to
be forgotten.

Ever yours most affectionately

Charles Dickens.

Wednesday Morning

May 1835

Monsieur Heger

No 32 Rue d'Isabelle

Bruxelles

Belgique

'... truly I find it difficult to be cheerful so long as I think I shall never see you more'

In February 1842 Charlotte and Emily Brontë travelled to Brussels to study languages at the boarding school run by Professor Constantin Héger and his wife, Mme Héger. In return for their board and tuition, Charlotte taught English and Emily taught music. In October 1842 their studies were cut short by the death of their Aunt Elizabeth Branwell, who had cared for the Brontë household and children since the premature death of their mother. Charlotte returned alone to Brussels in January 1843, but her second stay proved less happy than her first. Desperately homesick and lonely as well as increasingly infatuated with Professor Héger, Charlotte decided to leave in January 1844. Following her return to England, Charlotte wrote to the professor and incredibly four of her letters have survived, despite the fact that Professor Héger tore up three of them and threw all four away. Curiously, it is thanks to his wife – who retrieved them from the waste paper basket and sewed them back together – that we are privy to their content today. With the exception of one postscript, written in English, Charlotte wrote all four letters in French, the language that she associated with Héger. The letters are deeply poignant and reveal the extent of Charlotte's passionate feelings for the professor, her desire to see him, her despair at his silence and ultimately her resigned desolation and sense of rejection – emotions that she would later pour into *Jane Eyre* and *Villette*. 🖤

I must say one word to you in English – I wish I would write to you more cheerful letters, for when I read this over, I find it to be somewhat gloomy – but forgive me my dear master – do not be irritated at my sadness – according to the words of the Bible: 'Out of the fullness of the heart, the mouth speaketh' and truly I find it difficult to be cheerful so long as I think I shall never see you more. You will perceive by the defects in this letter that I am forgetting the French language – yet I read all the French books I can get, and learn daily a portion by heart – but I have never heard French spoken but once since I left Brussels – and then it sounded like music in my ears – every word was most precious to me because it reminded me of you – I love French for your sake with all my heart and soul.

Farewell my dear master – may God protect you with special care and crown you with peculiar blessings. CB

November 18th,
Haworth, Bradford, Yorkshire.

ommeil – je dépéris

P'ois-je vous écrire encore au mois de M[ai]
j'aurais voulu attendre toute une année – mais c'[est im-]
possible – c'est trop long.

C Brontë

I must say one word to you in English – I wish I [could]
write to you more cheerful letters, for when I read [it]
I find it to be somewhat gloomy – but forgive me my
master – do not be irritated at my sadness – according to [the words]
of the Bible "Out of the fullness of the heart, the mo[uth speaketh"]
and truly I find it difficult to be cheerful so long as [I think]
I shall never see you more. You will perceive by [the fault]
in this letter that I am forgetting the French language [– yet I]
read all the French books I can get, and learn da[ily a portion]
by heart – but I have never heard it French spoken [but once]
since I left Brussels – and then it sounded like [music in]
my ears – every word was most precious to me bec[ause it]
reminded me of you – I love French for your sake [with]
all my heart and soul.

Farewell my dear master – may God protect you [with special]
care and crown you with peculiar blessings

18th   CB.

Haworth   Bradford   Yorkshire

H. M. Prison.
Reading.

Dear Bosie,

After long and fruitless waiting I have determined to write to you myself, as much for your sake as for mine, as I would not like to think that I had passed through two long years of imprisonment without ever having received a single line from you, or any news or message even, except such as gave me pain.

Our ill-fated and most lamentable friendship has ended in ruin and public infamy for me, yet the memory of our ancient affection is often with me, and the thought that loathing, bitterness and contempt should for ever take that place in my heart once held by love is very sad to me: and you yourself will, I think, feel in your heart that to write to me as I lie in the loneliness of prison-life is better than to publish my letters without my permission or to dedicate poems to me unasked, though the world will know nothing of whatever words of grief or passion, of remorse or indifference you may choose to send as your answer or your appeal.

I have no doubt that in this letter in which I have to write of your life and of mine, of the past and of the future, of sweet things changed to bitterness and of bitter things that may be turned into joy, there will be much that will wound your vanity to the quick. If it prove so, read the letter over and over again till it kills your vanity. If you find in it something of which you feel that you are unjustly accused, remember that one should be thankful that there is any fault of which one can be unjustly accused. If there be in it one single passage that brings tears to your eyes, weep as we weep in prison where the day no less than the night is set apart for tears. It is the only thing that can save you. If you go complaining to your mother, as you did with reference to the scorn of you I displayed in my letter to Robbie, so that she may flatter and soothe you back into self-complacency or conceit, you will be completely lost. If you find one false excuse for yourself, you will soon find a hundred, and be just what you were before. Do you still say, as you said to Robbie in your answer, that I "attribute unworthy motives" to you? Ah! you had no motives in life. You had appetites merely. A motive is an intellectual aim. That you were "very young" when our friendship began? Your defect was not that you knew so little about life, but that you knew so much. The morning dawn of boyhood with its delicate bloom, its clear pure light, its joy of innocence and expectation you had left far behind. With very swift and running feet you had passed from Romance to

'After long and fruitless waiting I have determined to write to you myself, as much for your sake as for mine'

In 1895, the same year in which Oscar Wilde reached the height of his fame and success, with *An Ideal Husband* and *The Importance of Being Earnest* being performed on the stage in London, the writer was sentenced to two years' hard labour for homosexual offences. In 1884 Wilde had married Constance Lloyd, who bore him two sons, but some time in 1891 he met and fell in love with Lord Alfred Douglas, known to friends and family as Bosie. Their affair had disastrous consequences for Wilde, who, after being publicly insulted by Lord Alfred's father, the ninth Marquess of Queensberry, sued for criminal libel, triggering a chain of events that led to his imprisonment and public disgrace. Shown here are the first and last pages of 'De Profundis', the 50,000-word letter that Wilde wrote to Douglas from Reading Gaol between December 1896 and March 1897. As well as charting Wilde's spiritual growth through the physical and emotional hardships of his imprisonment, the letter is a bitter indictment of the man who he felt had helped to destroy his life and reputation. It is also one of the great love letters of history, in which Wilde acknowledges that even though 'our ill-fated and most lamentable friendship has ended in ruin and public infamy for me, yet the memory of our ancient affection is often with me, and the thought that loathing, bitterness and contempt should for ever take that place in my heart held by love is very sad to me'. 💚

H.M. Prison, Reading

Dear Bosie,

After a long and fruitless waiting I have determined to write to you myself, as much for your sake as for mine, as I would not like to think that I had passed through two long years of imprisonment without ever having received a single line from you, or any news or message even, except such as gave me pain.

Our ill-fated and most lamentable friendship has ended in ruin and public infamy for me, yet the memory of our ancient affection is often with me, and the thought that loathing, bitterness and contempt should for ever take that place in my heart once held by love is very sad to me: and you yourself will, I think, feel in your heart that to write to me as I lie in the loneliness of prison-life is better than to publish my letters without my permission or to dedicate poems to me unasked, though the world will know nothing of whatever words of grief or passion, of remorse or indifference you may choose to send as your answer or your appeal.

I have no doubt that in this letter in which I have to write of your life and mine, of the past and of the future, of sweet things changed to bitterness and of bitter things that may be turned into joy, there will be much that will wound your vanity to the quick. If it prove so, read the letter over and over again till it kills your vanity. If you find in it something of which you feel that you are unjustly accused, remember that one should be thankful that there is any fault of which one can be unjustly accused. If there be in it one single passage that brings tears to your eyes, weep as we weep in prison where the day no less than the night is set apart for tears. It is the only thing that can save you. [...] Your defect was not that you knew so little about life, but that you knew so much. The morning dawn of boyhood with its delicate bloom, its clear pure light, its joy of innocence and expectation you had left far behind. With very swift and running feet you had passed from Romance to Realism. The gutter and the things that live in it had begun to fascinate you. That was the origin of the trouble in which you sought my aid. [...]

At the end of a month when the June roses are in all their wanton opulence, I will, if I feel able, arrange through Robbie to meet you in some quiet foreign town like Bruges, whose grey houses and green canals and cool still ways had a charm for me, years ago. [...] I hope that our meeting will be what a meeting between you and me should be, after everything that has occurred. In old days there was always a wide chasm between us, the chasm of achieved art and acquired culture: there is a still wider chasm between us now, the chasm of Sorrow: but to Humility there is nothing that is impossible, and to Love all things are easy. [...]

What lies before me is my past. I have got to make myself look on that with different eyes, to make the world look on it with different eyes, to make God look on it with different eyes, this I cannot do by ignoring it, or slighting it, or praising it, or denying it. It is only to be done by fully accepting it as an inevitable part of the evolution of my life and character: by bowing my head to everything that I have suffered. How far I am away from the true temper of soul, this letter in its changing, uncertain moods, its scorn & bitterness, its aspirations & its failure to realise those aspirations, shows you quite clearly. But do not forget in what a terrible school I am sitting at my task. And incomplete, imperfect, as I am, yet from me you may have still much to gain. You came to me to learn the Pleasure of Life and the Pleasure of Art. Perhaps I am chosen to teach you something much more wonderful, the meaning of Sorrow, and its beauty,

Your affectionate friend, Oscar Wilde

... to rain ... and indeed it made ... sound like the name of a flower — you will have to surrender ... just so musical in its mouth of Fame, ... so sick to ... me, or my name, once ... ... will have to be abandoned by me, in turn. How narrow, and mean, and inadequate to its burden this ... Expression, is! It can give to Success its palace of Sorrow and Shame — it does not keep — even a wattled house in which they may dwell: all it can do for me is to bid me whisper my name into some other name, where mediaevalism would have given us the cowl of the monk, or the face-cloth of the leper behind which I might ... be at peace ..... I hope that our meeting ... ... will be what a meeting between you and me should be, after everything that has occurred. In old days there was always a wide chasm between us, the chasm of achieved Art and acquired culture: there is a still wider chasm, between us, the chasm of Sorrow: but to Humility there is nothing that is impossible, and to Love all things are easy.

As regards your letter to me in answer to this, it may be as long or as short as you choose. Address the envelope to 'the Governor. H.M. Prison. Reading': inside, in another, and an open envelope, place your own letter to me: if your paper is very thin do not write on both sides, as it makes it hard for others to read. I have written to you with perfect freedom. You can write to me with the same. What I must know from you is why you have never made any attempt to write to me, since the August of the year before last, more especially after, in the May of last year, ten months ago now, you knew, and admitted to others that you knew, how he had made me suffer, and how I realised it. I waited month after month to hear from you. Even if I had not been waiting but had shut the door against you, you should have remembered that no one can possibly shut the door against Love for ever. The unjust Judge in the Gospels rises up at length to give a just decision because Justice comes knocking daily at his door: at night-time, and the friend, in whose heart there is no real friendship, yields at length to his friend "because of his importunity." There is no prison in any world into which Love cannot force an entrance. If you did not understand that, you did not understand anything about Love at all. Then, let me know all about your article on me for the Mercure de France. I know something of it. You had better quote from it. It is set up in type. Also, let me know the exact terms of your Dedication. If it is in prose, quote the prose; if in verse, quote the verse. I have no doubt that there will be beauty in it. Write to me with full frankness about yourself: about your life: your friends: your occupations: your books. Tell me about your volume and its reception. Whatever you have to say, say it without fear. Don't write what you don't mean: that is all. If anything in your letter is false or counterfeit I shall detect it by the ring at once. It is not for nothing, or to no purpose, that in my life-long cult of literature I have made myself

Miser of sound and syllable, no less than Midas of his coinage.

Remember, too, that I have yet to know you. Perhaps we have yet to know each other.

For yourself, I have but this last thing to say. Do not be afraid of the past. If people tell you that it is irrevocable, do not believe them. The past, the present and the future are but one moment in the sight of God, in whose sight we should try to live. Time and space, succession and extension, are merely accidental conditions of Thought. The Imagination can transcend them, and move in a free sphere of ideal existences. Things, also, are in their essence what we choose to make them. A thing is, according to the mode in which one looks at it. Where others, says Blake, see but the Dawn coming over the hill, I see the sons of God shouting for joy. What seemed to the world and to myself my future I lost irretrievably when I let myself be taunted into taking the action against your father: had I, I dare say, lost it really long before that. What lies before me is my past. I have got to make myself look on that with different eyes, to make the world look on it with different eyes, to make God look on it with different eyes. This I cannot do by ignoring it, or slighting it, or praising it, or denying it. It is only to be done by fully accepting it as an inevitable part of the evolution of my life and character: by bowing my head to everything that I have suffered. How far I am away from the true temper of soul, this letter in its changing, uncertain moods, its scorn and bitterness, its aspiration and its failure to realise that aspiration, shows you quite clearly. But do not forget in what a terrible school I am sitting at my task. And incomplete, imperfect, as I am, yet from me you may have still much to gain. You came to me to learn the Pleasure of Life and the Pleasure of Art. Perhaps I am chosen to teach you something much more wonderful, the meaning of Sorrow, and its beauty.

Your affectionate friend
Oscar Wilde

have always been, I beseech
never less than that; only
this letter, for then you wi
want it; and just say sof
yourself sometimes

"I have a friend across
I like him, but he love
And come to me on your ow
for I cannot do without you

True, you will be cons
my love; but let that assu
I shall never do anything
to you.

At any rate, once in
I feel blessed and made
having written myself dow
lover
Gordon Bottomley

'More private than the unshaped wish at the centre of your heart'

The Yorkshire poet and playwright Gordon Bottomley (1874–1948) was incapacitated by crippling ill health for most of his life. He accepted his condition as a 'fine opportunity to live a life of passionate, intense meditation and contemplation – a life of the spirit concentrated upon the nature and processes of spiritual creation, as that is manifested in the arts which is man's most permanent achievement'. His interest in the arts found a natural outlet in correspondence, and his letters to many of the leading artists, writers, theatre directors and composers of the day are now stored in 120 volumes at the British Library. Bottomley's archive also contains some 500 letters that he wrote to the artist Emily Burton from 1895, during their early friendship and engagement, until their marriage in 1905. Bottomley had a masterful way with words and wrote with drama and passion, qualities that can also be found in this beautifully written letter from October 1899 in which he finally revealed his feelings to Emily. The couple lived most of their married life in Silverdale, near Carnforth in Lancashire. When Emily died in 1947, Bottomley was lost without her selfless and devoted companionship and outlived her by less than a year. 🌱

Well Knowe   *October 17th, 1899*

Dear My Lady

I can bear no longer to simulate a friendship for you which is less than what I feel; ever since I have known you I have had a thing in my heart to say to you, and in April last I determined to say it some day.

For a long time I thought it was my duty to leave this thing unsaid; so I did my duty, and it made me cross and irritable and bad-tempered to everyone, and, I fear, unkind even to you.

O, how I hope that I am not estranging you even when I tell you that I love you wholly, that as long as I have known you, you have been to me 'half angel and half bird and all a wonder and a wild desire', that your influence alone can waken what is best in me, that if I had not been penniless and helpless and

dependent upon my parents I should long ago have asked you to marry me.

(That poem Green Coif is as much about you as if it had your name for its title, and is and always was as much addressed to you as this letter is.)

But at one time I thought you were likely to marry a Liverpool artist-friend, a man of a finer and rarer spirit than I am; a man who would give you the life-atmosphere you need; and I loved you well enough to know how far more excellent this was than anything I could give you.

However, I have since thought that if you love him my speaking cannot draw you away from him; and that if your heart turns to me more than to other men (as my heart turns to you and to no other woman) then my keeping silent will not make you love him.

But how uncouthly, nay, barbarically, I have shown my love for you.

Ah, you think me a better and an abler man than I am; my one good-deed has been to recognize and reverence a great-hearted crystal-souled woman until she has become my true inspiration; this letter is the best poem I shall ever write in all my life.

I love you; I do not know how to say anything else.

If you care for me in this way, you will tell me, won't you?

But if this is all a mistake, if you can be no more to me than the friend you have always been, I beseech you to be never less than that; only, burn this letter, for then you will not want it; and just say softly to yourself sometimes

'I have a friend across the sea
I like him, but he loves me'

And come to me on your own terms, for I cannot do without you.

True, you will be conscious of my love; but let that assure you I shall never do anything distasteful to you.

At any rate, once in eternity I feel blessed and made glorious, having written myself down your lover.

Gordon Bottomley.

Well Knowe.   Oct. 14th. 1899

Dear My Lady,
        I can bear no longer to simula
a friendship for you which is less
than what I feel; ever since I
have known you I have had a thin
in my heart to say to you, and in
April last I determined to say it
some day.
        For a long time I thought
was my duty to leave this thing
unsaid; so I did my duty, and it
made me cross and irritable an
bad-tempered to everyone, and I
fear, unkind even to you.
        O, how I hope that I am not
estranging you when I tell you th
I love you wholly, that as long
I have known you you have be
to me "half-angel and half bir
And all a wonder and a wild desi
that your influence alone can wak
what is best in me, that if I ha
not been penniless and helpless an
dependent upon my parents I sho
long ago have asked you to
marry me.

Pages 1 and 2
of letter
from Gordon
Bottomley to
Emily Burton,
17 October 1899

(That poem Green Corf is as much about you as if it had your name for its title and is and always was as much addressed to you as this Letter is.

But at one time I thought you were likely to marry a Liverpool artist-friend, a man of a finer and rarer spirit than I am a man who would give you the life-atmosphere you need; and I loved you well enough to know how far more excellent this was than anything I could give you.

However, I have since thought that if you love him my speaking cannot draw you away from him; and that if your heart turns to me more than to other men (as my heart turns to you and to no other woman) then my keeping silent will not make you love him.

But how uncouthly, nay barbarically, I have shewn my love for you.

Ah, you think me a better and an abler man than I am; my one good deed has been to recognize and reverence a great-hearted crystal-souled woman until she has become my true inspiration; this letter is the best poem I shall ever write in all my life.

I love you; I do not know how to say anything else.

If you care for me in this way you will tell me, won't you?

XLIII

How do I love thee? Let me count the ways!—
I love thee to the depth & breadth & height
My soul can reach, when feeling out of sight
For the ends of Being and Ideal Grace.
I love thee to the level of everyday's
Most quiet need, by sun & candlelight—
I love thee freely, as men strive for Right;—
I love thee purely, as they turn from Praise!—
I love thee with the passion, put to use
In my old griefs;.. and with my childhood's faith
I love thee with the love I seemed to lose
With my lost Saints!— I love thee with the breath,
Smiles, tears, of all my life!— and, if God choose,
I shall but love thee better after death.

ELIZABETH BARRETT BROWNING,
SONNET 43 FROM *SONNETS FROM THE PORTUGUESE*
C.1846

'How do I love thee?
Let me count the ways'

Elizabeth Barrett was already a famous poet when, in January 1845, Robert Browning wrote to her and declared, 'I love your verses with all my heart, dear Miss Barrett.' She replied, 'I thank you Mr Browning from the bottom of my heart', and so began a correspondence that led to their first meeting and eventually to their engagement, which was carefully concealed from Elizabeth's tyrannical father. On 12 September 1846 the couple married in secret at St Marylebone parish church, and a week later eloped to Italy and settled in Florence, where Elizabeth remained until her death in 1861. Perhaps it was the birth of their son in 1849 that prompted Elizabeth to show her husband the collection of sonnets that she had secretly written during their courtship. They movingly describe the gradual flowering of her love for Robert. This is the manuscript draft of perhaps the most famous of them all, 'How do I love thee?' The title, *Sonnets from the Portuguese*, is a reference to Robert's nickname for his wife, 'my little Portuguese', derived from her poem 'Catarina to Camoens'. Robert Browning outlived Elizabeth Barrett by twenty-eight years, but never remarried, declaring that his heart was buried in Florence. 💘

How do I love thee? Let me count the ways.
I love thee to the depth and breadth and height
My soul can reach, when feeling out of sight
For the ends of Being and Ideal Grace.
I love thee to the level of everyday's
Most quiet need, by sun and candle-light.
I love thee freely, as men strive for Right;
I love thee purely, as they turn from Praise.
I love thee with the passion, put to use
In my old griefs, and with my childhood's faith.
I love thee with love I seemed to lose
With my lost saints – I love thee with the breath,
Smiles, tears, of all my life – and, if God choose,
I shall but love thee better after death.

1884.

Another year of joy & grief,
  Another year of hope & fear:
O Mother, is life long or brief?
  We hasten while we linger here.

But since we linger, love me still
  And bless me still, O Mother mine,
While hand in hand we scale life's hill,
  You Guide, & I your Valentine.

'The Queen of Hearts'

Christina Rossetti, one of the most important female poets of the Victorian period, is perhaps best remembered today for her beautiful Christmas carol, 'In the Bleak Midwinter'. Born in London in 1830, Christina was a precocious child and shared the artistic and intellectual interests of her brothers, the Pre-Raphaelite artist Dante Gabriel and the writer and critic William Michael. Her engagement to the painter James Collinson, who, like her brothers, was a member of the Pre-Raphaelite group of artists, poets and critics, was broken off with much anguish when he joined the Roman Catholic Church; Christina remained all her life a devout High Anglican. Ill health meant that she led a quiet and confined existence, living with her mother to whom she remained steadfastly loyal. This is one of eleven charming short poems that Christina wrote for her mother as 'Valentines' between 1876 and 1886. Each one is inscribed on the reverse 'The Queen of Hearts'. On a separate sheet a pencil note in the poet's hand explains: 'These Valentines had their origins from my dearest Mother's remarking that she had never received one. I, her CGR, ever after supplied one on the day; and (so far as I recollect) it was a surprise every time, she having forgotten all about it in the interim.'

my heart goes knocking when I think
of it. I don't understand —

Little child, I will kiss you till I kill you.
Be gentle with me.

                    Goodnight

                        Rupert

Do not answer anything.   I write this because
I like writing it   But answer points
of fact briefly.   it's a practical world

'I'm madly eager to see you again. My heart goes knocking when I think of it.'

In 2007 the British Library acquired a collection of eighty-two love letters written by the First World War poet Rupert Brooke to the English actress Cathleen Nesbitt. The previously unseen letters provide a fascinating insight into their two-year romance, which began when Brooke fell under Cathleen's spell while watching her performance as Perdita in *A Winter's Tale* at the Savoy Theatre in London. This letter, written in early 1913, shows how Brooke – once referred to by W.B.Yeats as 'the most handsome man in the country' – was captivated by Cathleen and worshipped 'her great beauty'. In another letter he wrote: 'Haven't you noticed your chin and neck are the most beautiful thing in the world? Haven't you heard about your hair? Has nobody told you about your eyes? Haven't you read in the papers that your lips are maddening?' Brooke bombarded her with marriage proposals and made frequent references to a life with 'lots of lovely children' away from the hustle and bustle of London. Brooke tragically died from blood poisoning on 23 April 1915, while on his way to fight in the fateful Gallipoli campaign. As if intuiting his approaching death, he wrote to Cathleen from 'off Gallipoli' on 18 March: 'Oh my dear, Life is a very good thing. Thank God I met you. Be happy and be good. You have been good to me. Goodbye, dearest child – Rupert.'

Pages 1 and 2 of letter from Rupert Brooke to Cathleen Nesbitt, 1913 out at a gentle rain. This evening I walked a few miles & smelt the hay. The country is very restful. I am more than ever suspicious of London. And you & your talk about the beauty of haggard faces & the ugliness of shining country skins — — .

"I bowed her foolish head,
And kissed her hair & laughed at her. Such a child
was she..."

as one of the Great Poets has written.

I hope you're happy & lovely tonight.

You must tell me where & how we meet on Tuesday. Pygmalion is it? I'll be up in the late afternoon (unless you want tea). Shall we dine at the Pall Mall, or in Soho — its fairly near?

My sweet child, my thoughts are full of you, all the day & night. I'm rather lonely — although you pretend to think, sometimes, that a life of luncheons & ballets &

Rugby   *Sunday*

My darling,

    I've been 'tidying' – putting away my letters for the last few weeks.
Yours among them. As I read them again, it seemed to me very wonderful that
you should be so good to me. Your loveliness comes out through your words …
I haven't deserved it. But I love you very much. [...]

    I've been writing sonnets all day and looking out at a gentle rain. This
evening I walked a few miles and smelt the hay. The country is very restful. I am
more than ever suspicious of London. And you and your talk about the beauty of

haggard faces and the ugliness of shining
country skies …

    'I bowed her foolish head, And kissed
her hair and laughed at her. Such a child
was she …' as one of the Great Poets has
written.

    I hope you are happy and lovely tonight.
You must tell me where and how we meet
on Tuesday. Pygmalion is it? I'll be up in the
late afternoon (when you want tea). Shall
we dine at the Pall Mall? Or in Soho – it's
fairly near?

    My sweet child, my thoughts are full
of you, all the day and night. I'm rather
lonely – although you pretend to think,
sometimes, that a life of luncheon and

ballets and suppers 'is all the human heart requires'. I'm a fool: but I do know that one needs other things. One thing I need – only one of many, but a strong one – oh! I know it is a great feebleness – is to worship. There aren't, these days, many things we can worship. I've found one: your great beauty. Thank God I found it.

Oh, but – it's the terrifyingly glad part of it – you're not only goddess; you're also child. Both at once: – what colour is shot silk? – That's what sends my blood beating to my head till I'm dizzy.

Cathleen, my darling, it is very wonderful when we're together. I wish to God you were coming in through the door now: and that I could hold your hands. There's beauty when we're together. I understand – in a way I understand you completely: because I love you so.

I'm madly eager to see you again. My heart goes knocking when I think of it. I don't understand ....

Little child, I will kiss you till I kill you. Be gentle with me.

Goodnight

Rupert

Do not answer lengthily. I write this because I like writing it. But answer points of fact briefly. It's a practical world.

My darling Eva

I don't quite know why
I am writing this — but one
never knows one's luck an
one can't say that one
is certain to come back
from an Enterprise such
as the one I hope to take
part in on Sunday
Morning — And so if we
are to part company, for
a bit, I want to tell you

'I want to tell you ... how blissfully happy I have been with you my Sweet Red Rose'

Sir Roger Keyes, one of the twentieth century's most important naval figures, enjoyed a distinguished career that spanned two world wars. Born in India on 4 October 1872, he joined the Royal Navy as a cadet in 1885 and when he married Eva Salvin on 10 April 1906 he had already reached the rank of Captain. Keyes served as Commander in charge of submarines from 1910 to 1914 and it was during this period, with England at war with Germany, that he wrote this letter to his wife and sealed it in an envelope marked 'Eva, Please do not open this until you hear of my death'. For obvious reasons, Keyes did not explain to his wife the nature of the enterprise that he was about to take part in, but history reveals that Keyes was preparing to join the Cuxhaven Raid, a particularly dangerous British ship-based air-raid on the Zeppelin sheds at Cuxhaven, originally scheduled for 11 December 1914 but then postponed until 25 December. Keyes survived the raid, returned home and the letter remained unopened. Years later, having retired from the navy as Admiral of the Fleet and been elevated to the peerage as Baron Keyes of Zeebrugge and Dover in 1943, he was sent on a goodwill mission to America, Canada, Australia and New Zealand. It was only then, in June 1944, that as a note added to the envelope by Eva Keyes reveals, the letter was 'opened at R[oger's] request before going round world'. 🦃

HMS Maidstone 10th December 1914

My darling Eva,

I don't quite know why I am writing this – but one never knows one's luck and
one can't say that one is certain to come back from an enterprise such as the one
I hope to take part in on Sunday morning – and so if we are to part company, for
a bit, I want to tell you before I go on my long journey how blissfully happy I have
been with you my Sweet Red Rose. It is hard to believe that this will be the end
of our partnership, and I will go in the hope that we will unite again in another
world. I know mine is the easier part, but I know you will show a gallant part
and live for those sweet babas – and the other to come. I would like you to ask
Reggie Tyrwhitt to be godfather – particularly mentioning the day this request
was written. I know you will always be sweet and kind to my mother and sister
– as you have ever been. Much as I would like to live to share many more happy
years with you darling, it is proper and right to be ready to die at such a time and
I know you will give me credit for going out very confidently and buoyantly to
meet my fate. May the God I believe in be with you and the babas always.
With all my love and all my thanks for your dear love.

I am your very devoted Roger.

10/12/14 · Roger

Eva.
Please do not open this
until you hear of my
death. Opened at R: request
before going round world June 1944
EK

My sweetest, my most dear darling Maeve

Today you will be going into the Nursing Home. I hope that everything will work smoothly & that everyone will be gentle to you, my dear little wife. I have had no definite news as to whether I can come or not but I will do my utmost. How wonderful it was to be able to talk to you last night, dear Maeve. As I told you, I was speaking from that family I told you about. They gave me high tea when I dropped in about 6 pm and I told them about yo

'You are in my heart, darling. I am loving you more than I have ever done before'

Mervyn Peake, best known today as the author of *Gormenghast*, was a uniquely talented artist and writer. Although he failed to shine academically, his creative gifts were apparent at an early age and nurtured by his teacher Eric Drake. After leaving school, Peake enrolled at Croydon School of Art and then briefly attended the Royal Academy Schools. In 1935 he was offered a teaching position at Westminster School of Art and it was here that he met the artist Maeve Gilmore, who had enrolled in sculpture classes. They married on 1 December 1937 and had two sons, Sebastian and Fabian, and a daughter, Clare. The first two decades of family life were spent in London, on Sark, in Kent and Surrey; later, in her memoir, *A World Away*, Maeve would recall these years as idyllic and marvellously fulfilling. From the middle of the 1950s Parkinson's disease gradually prevented Peake from working and led to his premature death in 1968. His archive, acquired by the British Library in 2010, includes a collection of personal letters from Peake to his wife. These were often, as the one received by Maeve just before she was due to give birth demonstrates, charmingly illustrated by the uxorious Peake. 🐦

My sweetest, my most dear darling Maeve,

Today you will be going into the nursing home. I hope that everything will work smoothly and that everyone will be gentle to you, my dear little wife. I have had no definite news as to whether I can come or not but I will do my utmost. How wonderful it was to be able to talk to you last night, dear Maeve. As I told you, I was speaking from that family I told you about. They gave me high tea when I dropped in about 6pm and I told them about you. I want to tell everyone about you – about your beauty – your sweetness, your paintings.

Are you feeling very imminent, Maeve. Do you feel worried or can you detach yourself at all. Oh darling, how I love you. How I love you.

Perhaps when this reaches you the little baby will be borne.

Oh Maeve. You are in my heart, darling. I am loving you more than I have ever done before. Bless you – oh my sweetheart, bless you. Bless you.

I am longing for your release. I am longing for news, and to be with you.

Maevie. I am in love. Deeply. Un-endingly, for ever and ever.

Your Mervyn

X

Cambridge was our courtship.
Not the colleges, or such precincts,
But everything from the Mill bridge
Towards Grantchester. Those river meadows,
Three or four square miles contained its
Ornaments with willows, + green level,
Full drooping willows + rushes, + mallard + swans,
Or stumpy pollard willows + the dank silence
Of the slippery lapsing Cam. That was our place.
Not spoiled by precedent, for either of us.
We walked on neat macadam on dusty paths,
And sat on benches + the skyline
All around was willows + cyclists — suspended,
In the watery weedy dream, the
An aquarium interval of slow
Waltzing figures, among glimpses
Of crumbling parapets, a horizon
Sinking below sea level. It was always dark.
One by one we made the public benches
Saved to us. What did we talk about?
The University was a delay, a sentence
To be borne out + escaped.
Our only life was to come. Suspended
We hung there, many or less, seeing
The scenery flow past like the silent river.
Were we actually going anywhere?
Were we exploring? Or talking away
Bewilderment, or trying word shapes
To make hopes visible. We talked.
What a locked garden the world seemed then,
When we walked past the gate, talking + talking.
We did not know what wings felt like.
Were what we felt wings?

'Cambridge was our courtship'

In late 2008, following the death of Ted Hughes, Poet Laureate and one of the most influential literary figures of the post-war generation, the British Library acquired all the papers remaining with his Estate. At the heart of this exceptional collection are the manuscripts relating to the volume *Birthday Letters*, Hughes's collection of poems that chart and explore his relationship with the poet Sylvia Plath, whom he met in February 1956 while both were studying in Cambridge. They married in June the same year and had two children, Frieda in 1960 and Nicholas in 1962, but by the time of Plath's suicide in 1963, she and Hughes had already separated. Hughes always remained resolutely silent on his life with Plath and her suicide, until 1995, when a small selection of the 'Birthday Letters' poems were unveiled in 'New Selected'. Then in 1998, Hughes published *Birthday Letters*, a series of eighty-eight powerful and intimate poems, written over a twenty-five-year period, about his troubled relationship with Plath and his reaction to her death. The poems are written in an open, tender, conversational language that addresses Plath directly. In this previously unpublished poem, Hughes reflects on their early courtship in Cambridge. *Birthday Letters* received widespread critical acclaim and a number of literary honours, including the T. S. Eliot prize for poetry and the Whitbread Book of the Year. 🍒

Cambridge was our courtship.
Not the colleges, or such precincts,
But everything from the Millbridge
Towards Grantchester. Those river meadows,
Three or four square miles contained it
Ornamented with willows, & green levels,
Full drooping willows & rushes, & mallard, & swans,
Or stumpy pollard willows & the dank silence
Of the slipping lapsing Cam. That was our place,

Not spoiled by precedent, for either of us.
We walked on neat macadam, on dusty paths,
And sat on benches & the skyline
All around was willows & cyclists – suspended,
In the watery, weedy, dream,
An aquarium interval of slow
Waltzing figures, among glimpses
Of crumbling parapets, a horizon
Sinking below sea level. It was always dark.
One by one we made the public benches
Sacred to us. What did we talk about?
The University was a delay, a sentence
To be borne with & escaped.
Our only life was to come. Suspended
We hung there moving our legs, seeing
The scenery flow past like the silent river,
Were we actually going anywhere?
Were we exploring? Or talking away
Bewilderment, or trying word-shapes
To make hopes visible. We talked.
What a locked garden the world seemed then,
When we walked past the gate, talking & talking.
We did not know what wings felt like.
Were what we felt wings?

26 Jan 70

Dearest Fernety,

Love

and many happy
returnes.

R.

'Dearest Ferrety'

Sir Ralph Richardson was one of the foremost stage and screen actors of his generation. He was born in 1902 in Cheltenham, Gloucestershire, where his father was art master at Cheltenham Ladies' College. He started his working life as an office boy for the Liverpool and Victoria Insurance Company in Brighton and then spent a short time at Brighton Art College, before deciding that he wanted to become an actor. On 18 September 1924 Richardson married the seventeen-year-old student-actress Muriel ('Kit') Hewitt. The following year the newlyweds joined the Birmingham Repertory Company, and Richardson made his first stage appearance in London for the Greek Play Society on 10 July 1926 as the stranger in *Oedipus at Colonus*. In 1927 Kit tragically contracted the disease Encephalitis lethargica, commonly known as 'sleeping sickness', and died in 1942 after a long illness. Richardson remarried on 26 January 1944. His new wife was Meriel ('Mu') Forbes, a member of the theatrical Forbes-Robertson family; their son Charles, known as 'Smallie', was born the following year. In 2002 the British Library purchased the papers and correspondence of Sir Ralph Richardson, including a large number of love letters and notes to his wife as 'Ferret' or 'Ferrety', a selection of which are shown here. They bear eloquent witness to the acting knight's deep attachment to his wife. 🍏

DEAREST
FERRETY
WAVES OF LOVE...
from
BRIGHTON
13 SEPT 6th

25 June 1969

The Prescription
Lady Richardson
Chester Terrace, NW1
To be taken with love.

RR (Doctor)

Undated
Dearest Ferret,
This is to wish you many happy
returns – if I am unable to meet you –
the room is no 207.
Shall be back about 5 o'clock I expect.
Ask the people to put the beds
together.
R.

Title page: Detail of letter on frontispiece (see below)

Frontispiece: Detail of letter by Mervyn Peake to his wife, Maeve Gilmore, 17 August 1950. Add Ms 88931/13/3/1/3

14, 17: British Library, Papyrus 42

15: © The British Museum

16: © The British Museum

18, 20, 21: British Library, Add Ms 43490, f.23

19: British Library, Add Ms 35215, f.5

22: British Library, Egerton Ms 616, f.14

24: © Philip Mould Ltd / Bridgeman Art Library

25: © Philip Mould Ltd / Bridgeman Art Library

26: British Library, Stowe Ms 955, f.6

28: British Library, Stowe Ms 955, f.5v

29: British Library, Stowe Ms 955, f.17

30: British Library, Kings Ms 9, f.66v

32: British Library, Kings Ms 9, f.231v

33 (left): British Library, Stowe Ms 956, f.1v

33 (right): © Dean and Chapter of Ripon Cathedral

34: British Library, Lansdowne Ms 1236, f.9

36: © National Portrait Gallery

37: British Library, Royal Ms 2A xvi, f.3

38: British Library, Add Ms 74286, ff.33v

40, 41: British Library, Add Ms 74286, ff.33, 33v

42: British Library, 688.l.13, opp.p.51

43: British Library, Egerton Ms 2572, f.11

44, 47: British Library, Harley Ms 4762, f.14

46: Mary Baskerville, later Mary Scudamore, by Marcus Gheeraerts the Younger (1615), © National Portrait Gallery, London

48, 51: British Library, Add Ms 42153, f.5

50: British Library, 10922.g.1, f.p

52, 56, 57: British Library, Harley Ms 6987, ff.157, 158

54: British Library, 193.a.1, f.p

55: British Library, 688.l.13, opp.p.67

58: British Library, Add Ms 33975, f.60v

59: British Library, 10906.dd.23, f.p

61: British Library, 688.l.13, opp.p.133

62, 66, 67: British Library, Add Ms 47608, ff.67, 68, 68v

64: Lady Mary Fenwick in mourning dress, holding a miniature of her husband, © Fitzwilliam Museum, Cambridge

65: British Library, 9503.h.1, p.102

68, 71: British Library, Add Ms 39839, f.42

69: British Library 10862.ee.34, pl.iv

70: British Library 010854.G.11, opp.p.178

72: British Library, Egerton Ms 1614, f.125

73: © National Maritime Museum

74: British Library, 10825.b.45, f.p

74, 75: British Library, Egerton Ms 1614, ff.125v, 126

76, 80, 81: British Library, Add Ms 43689, ff.2, 3v

78: British Library, Dexter 316/126 (detail)

79: Private Collection / Bridgeman Art Library

82: British Library, Add Ms 38732D

84: British Library, B.511876, p.22 (top) and Brussels Brontë Society (bottom)

85: British Library, Add Ms 38732C

86, 91: British Library, Add Ms 50141A, ff.1, 40v

90: British Library, c.131.f.11

92–97: British Library, Add Ms 88957/1/1

98: British Library, Add Ms 43487, f.49

101: British Library, 1162.h.2, f.p. and 1203.g.3, opp.p.52

102: British Library, Ashley Ms 1376, f.16

103: British Library, 010920.f.20, f.p

104: British Library, Add Ms 83315, f.52v

106, 107: British Library, Add Ms 83315, ff.51, 51v

108: © National Portrait Gallery, London, photo by Bassano

109: Private Collection / Ken Welsh / Bridgeman Art Library

110: British Library, Add Ms 82391

113: British Library, 01087.l.4, p.358, f.p. and Add Ms 82391 (envelope)

114–117: British Library, Add Ms 88931/13/3/1/1

118: British Library, Add Ms 88918

120: Mortimer Rare Book Room, Smith College, USA, and the Estate of Ted Hughes

122–124: British Library, Ralph Richardson Archive, Add Ms 82066-67

TEXT CREDITS

Text © Andrea Clarke, 2011

The British Library would like to thank the following for their kind permission to reproduce letters in this book:

85: (Oscar Wilde, *De Profundis*), Merlin Holland

103: (Rupert Brooke to Cathleen Nesbitt), Professor Jon Stallworthy

109: (Roger Keyes to his wife Eva), Josa Young

113: (Mervyn Peake to his wife, Maeve Gilmore), The Estate of Mervyn Peake

117: (Ted Hughes, 'Cambridge was our courtship'), The Estate of Ted Hughes

121: (Letters from Ralph Richardson to his wife, Meriel Forbes), The Trustees of The Ralph and Meriel Richardson Foundation

ACKNOWLEDGEMENTS

The author would like to thank the following
for their invaluable assistance:
Jamie Andrews, Claire Breay, Helen Broderick, Julian Harrison,
Arnold Hunt, Kathryn Johnson, Scot McKendrick,
Jill Purslow, Lara Speicher, Michael St John-McAlister, Zoe Wilcox

First published in 2011 by
The British Library
96 Euston Road, London NW1 2DB

Cataloguing in Publication Data
A catalogue record for this book is available from The British Library
ISBN 978 0 7123 5825 5

Designed by Andrew Barron
Colour reproductions by Dot Gradations Ltd, Essex
Printed in Hong Kong by Great Wall Printing Co. Ltd